PRAISE FOR *MARY MAC*

M000287880

"We can feel Mary's energy leapii. words here are part of a pure transmission of Mary's teaching that is now being restored to the world. If you want to hear the real voice of Mary Magdalene, buy this book."

—Stuart Wilson and Joanna Prentis, authors of
Power of the Magdalene, *The Essenes*, and *The Magdalene Version*

"*Mary Magdalene Beckons* brings forth perennial wisdom teachings of the Sacred Feminine in conscious partnership with the Sacred Masculine, through the love story of Mary Magdalene and Jesus Christ. The philosophy of loving connectedness between all things is at the heart of original Christianity and is brought forth once again through Mercedes Kirkel's articulated connection with Mary Magdalene. Many are searching for the characteristics of Mary Magdalene that will be useful for us as we build a better world together. Mercedes gives us an intelligent and 'feelingful' Magdalene who can guide us through transformative processes into greater light and deeper love."

—Joan Norton, author of *The Mary Magdalene Within* and
(with Margaret Starbird) *14 Steps to Awaken the Sacred Feminine*

"*Mary Magdalene Beckons* is a beautiful book of inspirational teach-ings. The duo formed by a spiritual being and an experienced spiritual practitioner gives the teachings a very practical slant. The perspective offered in this book will help many to understand and to fully participate in the shift of consciousness."

—Sophie Rose, author of channeled course
The Way of the Heart, Teachings of Jeshua and Mary Magdalene

"Mercedes Kirkel has eloquently recorded and explained a very important set of messages in *Mary Magdalene Beckons*. After each message from Mary, Mercedes shares her own insights, allowing the reader to build a bridge between spirit beings and human beings on Earth. I recommend *Mary Magdalene Beckons* to help us understand the hows and whys of our common predicament as human beings seeking to end the illusion of separation from God and to free ourselves and return to love."

—Sal Rachele, author of *Earth Awakens* and *Earth Changes and 2012*

"Mercedes Kirkel's straightforward receptivity to and wise commentary on Mary Magdalene's revelations are sure to be of tremendous help to many people who are ready to integrate the Divine Feminine in their hearts, souls, and lives. If these teachings are right for you, they will help you transform your relationship to elements of life that you might have considered 'unspiritual'—such as pain, difficult feelings, and the whole realm of sexuality. And through that transformation, you'll come closer both to God and your own freedom, wholeness, and intrinsic joy."

—Saniel Bonder, author of
Healing the Spirit/Matter Split, While Jesus Weeps, and *Ultimaya 1.0*

"In this book, Mercedes Kirkel channels Mary Magdalene and expounds on Mary's keen wisdom. I especially like Mary's invitation to open our hearts to pain and to understand our deeper Feminine Divine nature. I highly recommend this reading for anyone who wants to understand the Feminine Divine within him- or herself."

—Marcia McMahon, author of *With Love from Diana, Queen of Hearts*

"In *Mary Magdalene Beckons*, Mercedes Kirkel shares valuable practical insights on how we can live our best life where the rubber meets the road. This book takes us on a colorful and thought-provoking journey."

—Rev. Brendalyn Batchelor, minister, Unity Santa Fe

MARY MAGDALENE BECKONS

MARY MAGDALENE
BECKONS
Join the River of Love

Mercedes Kirkel

FOREWORD BY FLO AEVEIA MAGDALENA

INTO THE HEART
Creations
SANTA FE, NEW MEXICO

Published by:

Into the Heart Creations
PO Box 32742
Santa Fe, NM 87594
www.intotheheart.org

Book design by Angela Werneke

Cover art by Toni Chiapelli, with Teri Yarbrow, Max Almy, and Angela Werneke

Cover background: Swan Nebula, courtesy of NASA, ESA, and J. Hester (ASU)

The following illustrations are courtesy of Karuna Arts Inc., www.karunaarts.com: Chakra Goddess (figure 1-1); Shakti Dancing (figure 5-1); and Yab-Yum (figure 6-2).

The following illustrations are courtesy of the Center for Nonviolent Communication, © 2005 by Center for Nonviolent Communication, website: www.cnvc.org, email: cnvc@cnvc.org, phone: +1.505–244–4041: Needs Inventory (figure 2-1); Feelings Inventory (figure 9-1).

First edition

Printed in the United States of America

Publisher's Cataloging-in-Publication Data

Kirkel, Mercedes.

    Mary Magdalene beckons : join the river of love / Mercedes Kirkel. — 1st ed. — Santa Fe, N.M. : Into the Heart Creations, c2012.

    p. ; cm.

    ISBN: 978-0-9840029-5-5

    1. Mary Magdalene, Saint. 2. Spirit writings. 3. Spiritual life. 4. Spirituality. 5. New Age movement. 6. Jesus Christ—New Age movement interpretations. 7. Jesus Christ—Family. 8. Channeling (Spiritualism) I. Mary Magdalene, Saint (Spirit) II. Title.

BS2485 .K57 2012	2011938333
226/.092—dc23	1206

1 3 5 7 9 10 8 6 4 2

To all beings everywhere
who are reaching for light and love,
and to all those who help us.

Acknowledgments

I'M GRATEFUL beyond words to all the people I've shared Mary's messages with, who responded so deeply from their hearts. Seeing the looks of inspiration on your faces and love in your eyes has given me the fuel to do so many things I've never done before in order that you and many others can have this book. Thank you, from my heart to yours.

I feel deep appreciation for all my teachers and guides who have helped me develop the inner foundation upon which Mary's messages rest. Thank you to Marshall Rosenberg for your groundbreaking work around feelings and their relationship to needs. And I thank Tom Kenyon and Judi Sion, whose book opened this chapter of my life, and Ariya Lorenz, who knew I needed to read it.

I'm so grateful to my wonderful circle of friends—Christy Ceraso, Amara Karuna, Rose Messenger, Raydiance Grace, Andrea Pro, Elaine Oliveri, and many others—who supported me and believed in me as I opened to communicating with beings of light. Thank you to Monsignor Olona, who held a light for me in my relationship with Mary when I desperately needed faith and trust. Thank you to my dad and stepmom, Hugh and Marjorie Kirkel, who listened with open minds and hearts to my sharing of the messages as they came through. And a huge thanks to my dear friend and spiritual companion Cliff Bain, who has been my cheerleader throughout this process and never ceased to believe in me and in this work.

I have deep appreciation for all my editors—Jude Byrne, Nancy O'Connor, Stuart Wilson, Sarah Aschenbach, and Barbara Doern Drew—whose unflagging encouragement and skillful polishing have contributed immensely to bringing this book to completion and making it shine. Ellen Kleiner has been my "fairy godmother" in guiding the book from my original manuscript to its fully manifest form. I'm also grateful to Amara Karuna, whose beautiful illustrations have contributed to the book. And I have tremendous gratitude to Angela Werneke, whose deep artistic sensitivity and talent so perfectly captured the beauty of Mary's messages in the book design, cover, and illustrations. Angela was also instrumental in helping to create the image of Mary for the cover, which was a most magical cocreative process between artists Toni Chiapelli, Teri Yarbrow, Max Almy, and Angela—under Mary's guidance.

And last, but really first, another thanks to my dad for instilling in me the belief that I can do anything I set my mind to. To my mom, Marjorie Young, and my daughter, Manger Huebner, who are the manifestations of the Divine Feminine in my life, I love you and thank you for sharing this journey of life with me. And to Mary, I am forever grateful for what you have brought to me and to the world.

Contents

PART IV ~ A NEW WAY OF RELATING TO LIFE

PART V ~ THE GREATNESS BEYOND THE MIND

PART VI ~ MARY SHARES OF HERSELF

PART VII ~ THE CALL TO ALL HEARTS

Illustrations

Foreword

A Banquet for the Soul! A Treasure for the Heart!

MARY MAGDALENE is one of Jesus's most mysterious and celebrated disciples. Numerous authors, lecturers, researchers, and ministers have depicted her in a variety of ways, ranging from a controversial, somewhat maligned figure to a wise and powerful ally of Christ who helped shape his ministry. No matter how she is viewed, however, the story of Mary Magdalene is one of a courageous, determined, and resilient woman whose light is so bright it has not been extinguished in over two thousand years.

With *Mary Magdalene Beckons*, Mercedes Kirkel brings this bright light to us in one of the most profound books of our day. *Mary Magdalene Beckons* offers heartfelt messages of understanding and guidance from the deeply committed soul of Mary Magdalene, urging us to cease feeling alone, separate, or disillusioned in the midst of life's challenges and to embrace hope instead of despair. Mercedes and Magdalene convey messages that are clear and deeply evocative, showing us how our desire for peace, harmony, and balance is fulfilled deep within us in the place of the Divine and how it can be accessed through our hearts.

Magdalene teaches us how to love by speaking about her life and learning. Her communications honestly and candidly reveal her deep love for Christ and the joy and commitment they created through their union. The subjects she addresses reflect dilemmas we have all faced and questions we have all pondered in these turbulent times. Knowing the human path of suffering, Magdalene leads us step-by-step from a condition of loss and pain to one of inner peace that restores our wisdom and unity with God. She shows us how to live without judgment, blame, or projection through experiencing oneness with our divine heart.

Magdalene not only provides us with pathways for resolving our innermost challenges, she walks the pathways with us. She understands the pain of living in our dualistic world. She describes the choices we have to foster either peace or conflict in our hearts. She brings messages of spiritual guidance that offer consolation and acceptance of our humanness. Her messages inspire us to remember that within our own hearts are divine seeds of compassion that bring understanding and release. In this way, Magdalene leads us to the place within ourselves where we are no longer adrift—where we're able to acknowledge our power and purpose and realize our capacity to live happy, full, and productive lives.

As Magdalene reveals a profound yet simple method for transforming our troubles and challenges, Mercedes illustrates the principles introduced by Magdalene with examples from her own life. These experiences from the current time help clarify the pathways Magdalene opens for us.

Once we have read their words, their message resides permanently in our consciousness, not to be refuted by the mind as other concepts are. The truths that the messages convey continually surface within and around the mind's thoughts, making it possible to remain open to the Divine—the key to the sanctuary of our souls and the pureness of our beings.

Mary Magdalene Beckons is a guide that can help all people connect to the source of their suffering and transform their pain into a joyful state of understanding, grace, and resolution. It is a resource for the heart and soul, pertinent to all people. Readers will return again and again to its trusted guidance that speaks to our

human condition and encourages us to persevere, to forgive ourselves, and to open to the heart of the One. When we access and
claim the Divine as our path, we are enfolded in our heart of hearts
and reside in the rhythm of creation, where "peace passeth understanding."

Flo Aeveia Magdalena
Putney, Vermont
April 2012

Flo Aeveia Magdalena is the author of
I Remember Union *and* Sunlight on Water

MARY MAGDALENE BECKONS

How This Book Came to Be
(Or "Why Me?")

IN THE SUMMER OF 2010, Mary Magdalene began communicating with me on a daily basis. Over the course of thirty days, I received twenty-five messages from her, each one packed with transformational wisdom. I knew right away these messages weren't intended just for me; rather, I was quite sure Mary wanted them to be communicated to many other people. By the end of the thirty days, she had clearly let me know that she wanted these messages to become a book—and that was the birth of this material.

Serving as Mary's representative on Earth presented me with a completely new role. One of my first questions was, "Why me? Why did Mary choose to communicate with me?" I imagine that you may also have this same question. In an attempt to provide an answer, I would like to share some of my life story.

I was born into a Jewish family that had only a nominal interest in participating in religious activities, and I grew up in the sixties in an all-Christian midwestern American town. This background gave me the interesting perspective of being surrounded by Christians and connected to Judaism through my family, while not feeling I was a part of either religion.

My earliest memory of a spiritual experience occurred when I was eight years old. My family had gone to the New York World's Fair that summer, and my mother very much wanted to visit the Vatican exhibit, where Michelangelo's *Pieta* was on display. While we waited in the long line, my mother did her best to explain to me what we were about to see, but I really didn't understand. Finally, we were ushered inside, where it was mostly dark except for the lights upon the art and so quiet you could hear a pin drop. As I viewed the beautiful statue of Mary holding the body of Jesus after he was crucified, I had a profound experience of moving into a transcendent state, a state I can feel in my body even as I write this. I didn't know what had happened, but afterward I could feel that my mother had experienced something similar.

Later that same year, I had my second spiritual experience. My birthday was approaching, and I remember the feeling of excited anticipation as I looked forward to that special occasion, which along with Christmas was the pinnacle of my life in those years. When the day finally arrived, I was celebrated in all the usual ways I had come to associate with birthdays. I had fun and felt loved by my family and friends; nevertheless, in the following days and weeks I remember a calm awareness—somewhere at the core of my being—of a subtle sense of nonfulfillment. Right then I consciously realized, "There must be more to life than this."

When I was twelve, images and memories began to surface of having been with Jesus in the desert. I clearly saw him being followed by about a hundred people, and I was one of them: a young woman, perhaps in her twenties. It never occurred to me to tell anyone about these memories, as I didn't think anyone would understand. I kept them to myself, and over time the images receded into the background of my memory.

During that same time, I became fascinated with East Indian traditional spirituality and started taking out books on Hinduism from the local library. The only ones that were available back then (at least in our small-town library) were scholarly texts, and although I couldn't understand most of what was presented, I was undaunted in my efforts to read and digest what I found. In my late teens and early twenties, my life path continued to include spirituality, first through studying the writings of Mahatma Gandhi and then through practicing hatha yoga, Indian meditation and chanting, and Zen Buddhism.

At twenty-one, I was introduced to the teaching of the American spiritual teacher Adi Da, and I became his formal devotee. I actively participated in the Adi Da spiritual community for seventeen years—meditating, studying, serving, living the life disciplines, birthing and raising a child, teaching in the community's spiritually based schools, and passionately engaging in the whole process.

In the midnineties, I moved on to another spiritual community, culminating my spiritual quest with Saniel Bonder in the Waking Down community. There I had a profound awakening into the unity of the two parts of reality that had always seemed fundamentally separate: my ordinary, mortal, limited self and my inherent Self-nature as infinite consciousness and unconditional love, nonseparate from all. I experienced a shift at the core of my being into a new sense of who I am, characterized by inner knowingness of my oneness with God. The sense of subtle disturbance that had previously driven my life dissolved in this fulfillment of my spiritual search.

After that spiritual awakening, I continued for another year as a teacher in the Waking Down process, helping others in their spiritual journey. During that time, a new sense of direction began to grow in me. I started yearning for greater connection with the earth and to be living in community with others who valued earth-based spirituality. I studied with a Native American shaman whose instructions awakened memories from previous lifetimes of engaging in the ancient pagan tradition of Goddess-based spirituality. I also studied belly dance, and the dances triggered memories of past lives as a temple dancer. My body *remembered* that the dance was a record of esoteric knowledge for awakening kundalini energy (spiritual energy that rises up the spine).

Around this time, I began having visions in which I was leading spiritual rituals at a beautiful lake and on the side of a volcano. In 1999, I moved to Hawaii, close to a gorgeous lake that looked just like the one in my visions and was less than an hour away from the actively erupting volcano of Kilauea. Over the next few years, my identity as a carrier of Tantric wisdom began to reveal itself. Tantra is an ancient spiritual path that reveals the unity of the Divine with all forms of manifest life, including sexuality. I'd been engaging in Tantric practices for twenty years, yet I'd never particularly focused on Tantra as special or unique. To me, it just seemed natural. However, during this time, I was introduced to many contemporary Tantra teachers and schools, and to my surprise I found that I generally already knew more about Tantra than what was being taught in these schools. I began remembering past lives as a temple priestess, during which I had taught and practiced the sacred path of union and ecstasy through mastery of sexual energy. It soon became clear to me that I had a mission to once again teach Tantra. But the form of Tantra I wanted to share with others differed from what was generally being promoted as Tantric sexuality: I wanted to emphasize the integration of sexuality—and all our human ordinariness—with awakened love and consciousness.

The year 2008 initiated the most recent chapter in my spiritual unfolding. At that time, a friend introduced me to a channeled book about Mary Magdalene, *The Magdalen Manuscript*, by Tom Kenyon and Judi Sion. In the book, Mary reveals that she was a priestess of Isis—a goddess worshipped in ancient Egypt—who was prepared for her relationship with Yeshua so that together they could engage in the sacred, esoteric practices of divine transformation. I was powerfully drawn to the practices she described and found myself immediately and easefully engaging in them. These practices activated a deep process of remembering as I connected with my own past as a priestess of Isis. My long-dormant memory of having been with Yeshua in the desert once again came to life, and I saw I had also known Mary Magdalene and Lady (Mother) Mary during that same time.

For the next year, I connected directly with Isis, who guided me to begin leading priestess-training groups. I didn't feel qualified to instruct others when I myself was just reawakening to my own priestess roots, but thankfully, prior to each group, Isis told me exactly what to do. The trainings turned out to be very powerful. In late 2009, I received a message from Spirit that I was to leave the Big Island of Hawaii, where I had lived for ten years. I was quite happy in Hawaii and thought I would live there for the rest of my life, so I checked the message out three times, wanting to be sure. The communication remained consistent, so I chose to follow it; I'd seen from past experiences that following Spirit's guidance always worked out for the best.

Thus, in spring of 2010, I headed for the mainland, not knowing where I was to settle. I spent six months traveling, spending time with my family, and visiting sacred sites. Eventually, I was guided to Santa Fe, New Mexico, where my heart felt ecstatically connected with the Sangre de Cristo ("Blood of Christ") mountains; I loved the amazing desert sky, highlighted with dramatic rays of light and vivid streaks of lightning; and I delighted in the warm colors and shapes of the adobe architecture, the vibrant multiethnic culture of art and music, and the great openness of the many people who embraced me there.

Within days of settling in Santa Fe, Mary Magdalene began coming to me every morning, bringing her impassioned messages about what we need to do at this moment to move forward in our spiritual evolution. I recorded these messages faithfully and watched as, over a month, she transmitted this book to me. The whole process seemed miraculous, and I knew without a doubt that sharing Mary's phenomenal wisdom with others was to be the new direction of my life.

In retrospect, it seems that much of what I'd done in my life up to that point had prepared me perfectly for the work of communicating Mary's teaching. However, I've been told by several psychics that I've been with Mary for many lifetimes, so it may be the other way around: perhaps my history with Mary influenced me—in this life—to make the particular choices I've made. Either way, I'm extremely grateful to be where I am now and to be the messenger for this body of work.

I believe we're living in a unique and powerful time of transformation, a time when more and more people are responding to the call of spiritual evolution. In the midst of this awakening process, I'm confident that Mary's guidance will be a tremendous help to untold numbers of people.

I feel enormously blessed to have received such a treasure, and it is my greatest honor to share it with you.

A Guide for Reading This Book

A NUMBER OF ASPECTS of this book may seem unusual, especially if you're not familiar with channeled material—information received telepathically from a being in another dimension. This explanatory section will help you understand specific elements that are relatively unique to this book, so that you can have the fullest access to the riches contained herein.

Mary's Voice and Mercedes's Voice

Each chapter begins with a message from Mary Magdalene. As I received these messages, I was consistently amazed at the perfect form of each communication and at Mary's brilliance and articulateness. I simply recorded what she was saying, and at the end of each transmission, I was left with a flawless communication.

Two other things stood out for me in Mary's transmissions. First was the energy that always accompanied her words. In relaying these messages, Mary not only communicated ideas and concepts, but she also shared her state of being. Receiving her energetic transmission was incredibly precious to me. I took it as a form of spiritual blessing, one that is quite potent for supporting growth and transformation. I believe the same blessing is available to all who receive her communication, including those who read this book. As you take in Mary's words, I urge you to open yourself fully to their power to bless and let yourself deeply experience her. Her blessing is one of her gifts, as is the wisdom she conveys and the practices she recommends.

The second thing I noticed was how much Mary was able to impart with so few words. Consistently eloquent and concise, she gracefully steered her discourse through vast amounts of information and profound understandings.

At some point as I was receiving these communications, Mary asked that I add my own explanations to her messages, along with personal stories, in order to support readers' understanding of what she was communicating. My sense was that she wanted me to unpack the meaning she was bringing forth to make sure that all her gems were given space to be absorbed. The process reminded me of spreading out a string of pearls so as to be able to contemplate each pearl, one at a time, and absorb its full beauty. I also understood that she wanted me to articulate the concepts in a less abstract style to supplement the richly laden, holistic-poetic form she uses. I have endeavored to do so in the commentary section following each of her messages.

The Sequence of the Messages

Each chapter is devoted to a separate message from Mary. I chose to present the messages in the order in which I received them, trusting Mary's choices and wisdom as to the progression of ideas. However, I made one exception: I moved what is now chapter fifteen, "The Consciousness of Inclusion," ahead of where it was in the original sequence because it was a continuation of the ideas that Mary began in chapter fourteen, "Lifting the Veil around Abundance and Death." I did this to make it easier to follow the development of Mary's concepts.

The Names Yeshua and Mary

In her messages, Mary always refers to Jesus as Yeshua. Many people believe that Yeshua was the Aramaic/Hebrew name for Jesus two thousand years ago in Israel, and I assume this is the name Mary knew him by. Because Yeshua is the name she used in her communications with me, I also refer to Jesus as Yeshua.

The only time Mary referred to herself in the messages was at the closing of each communication, when she simply said, "I AM Mary Magdalene," and once in chapter six ("My Sacred Relationship with Yeshua"). Accordingly, I chose to refer to her as Mary rather than use the Hebrew Miriam or the Aramaic Maryam. It occurs to me that she may have used the name Mary Magdalene because that is the name most people know her by today. I simply accept it as her choice.

Mary Magdalene's Personal Life

In her messages, Mary says very little about her own life or her life with Yeshua. I sense that this was intentional on her part. She was focused on helping us with our transformation now, not on what she did or didn't do two thousand years ago. I believe that Mary views the fascination with her historical life as a diversion from the truth and spiritual help that she and Yeshua offer. Truth and spiritual help were their focus at the time they were physically embodied on Earth, and that is why so many people responded to Yeshua. It's what ultimately matters with anyone we trust to guide us.

While I, as much as anyone else, would love to know the historical facts surrounding Yeshua's and Mary's lives, I believe Mary had a higher purpose in offering these messages. She wants to change the course of future history by helping us to change. I have personally experienced the transformative power of Mary's communications within myself and in my life. I invite you also to share in this experience through applying her wisdom to your life and observing the results. If you do so, I have great confidence that you will find immense value in Mary's instruction and transmission. You will also begin to develop your own personal relationship with Mary now, in the present, as I have done. I've come to value this relationship and her teachings much more than learning about her personal life.

Having said all that, I want to add that Mary does share some of her personal life—especially her life with Yeshua—in these messages, and I found those parts to be most beautiful and poignant. She seemed to sense when her sharing would help us to open our hearts and go deeper into the reality she's describing. It certainly had that effect on me, and I feel profound gratitude for all she chose to reveal.

Repetition of Ideas

You will probably notice some repetition of ideas throughout the messages. I believe that Mary repeats herself purposely in order to reinforce the things she is passionate for us to understand. Repetition gives us multiple opportunities to absorb her ideas at increasingly deeper levels. And the reiteration of concepts from previous messages also allows each message to be read as a complete communication unto itself.

Capitalization

I chose to capitalize words that are descriptions of the Divine. Capitalization is my way of trying to express in writing certain ideas and feelings that push the limits of language. For me, the capitalization visually communicates a sense of greatness and reverence, not in the religious sense but in the sense of that which is inherently sacred and profound. One example of this is the word *earth*. I capitalized *earth* at times to point to her spirit as a living, sentient being, the Divine Mother in one of her forms of manifestation—a very powerful form on this planet. At other times, *earth* is used in a more generic sense that does not require capitalization, except when referring to the planet Earth. Yet, my system of capitalization isn't perfect. Where I wasn't clear, I used my best judgment, realizing that everything is ultimately God manifesting in a particular form or circumstance.

My Adulation of Mary

I am sure it will be obvious as you read my commentaries that I hold Mary in highest regard. Many times throughout the manuscript, I voice my profound gratitude to her for what it's like for me to be in relationship with her and receive her gifts. I tried not to overdo this, because I could go on endlessly about the wonder I feel for her and the marvel of having her in my life. But I'd rather support you in discovering your own relationship with Mary and her teachings. My hope is that what I've written here will do that.

I've also had the sublime experience of channeling Yeshua. His energy feels very different from Mary's. I experience Yeshua as extremely powerful and exalted, immensely vulnerable, and profoundly sensitive. He doesn't seem to want to talk about the mundane, and I sense it takes a great effort for him to translate our mundane point of view into what is real and of value to him. By contrast, Mary seems supremely skilled in helping us with all aspects of our earthly experience while maintaining her complete centeredness and her divine calm of oneness with God. In this, Yeshua and Mary serve as the perfect archetypes of Masculine and Feminine, with Yeshua representing the transcendent and Mary the immanent. I have come to see Mary as a bridge, or mediator, between Yeshua and us.

How to Read This Book

I recommend initially reading the chapters in order, because there's a definite progression to Mary's ideas. She's building a specific understanding and practice, and she seems completely conscious of how she chooses to go about this. I see her messages taking us on a journey that leaves us changed at the end.

I can imagine people reading Mary's messages again and again, as different and deeper aspects are revealed with each reading. You may choose to reread certain chapters that call to you, or you may intuitively pick chapters to read, like picking a card from a Tarot deck. I trust you'll be guided to find the way that's best for you.

PART I

The Divine Feminine

ONE

Receiving the Divine Feminine

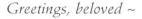

Greetings, beloved ~

I am here. Do not doubt my presence. Doubt is part of your mind.
I am here to help free you from your doubting mind.

    I have waited two thousand years to come forth, for the turning
of the ages when the Divine Feminine can be received, honored, and
reinstated in her rightful place as the equal partner and lover of the
Divine Masculine. There is much to be done for this to be accomplished, for the Divine Feminine has suffered much repression and
denial so that most are afraid of her and no longer know her. I am
here to help change that. This is the time for the Feminine to come
to the front, to lead in this progression into the new age. It is the
time of love and honoring of the Feminine, listening to the Feminine,
and allowing the Feminine to lead so that balance may be reestablished and we may become whole.

    And what does this mean for all of you? You are in the process
of learning to reconnect with, trust, and open to the Feminine within
yourself—as your body, your sexuality, your emotions. You are
learning to surrender your thinking to pure presence, to surrender
your lower mind to the heart. In doing this, the veils surrounding your
sacred mind can be lifted, and the marriage of the sacred heart and
sacred mind can occur. You are to celebrate that marriage through

the ongoing joy of bringing the light into your body, merging it with love, and sending this empowered love-light out into the world.

Many of you have become alienated from the Feminine within yourself. You've become afraid and cut off from your body and your emotions and your sexuality and your feeling heart. It will take practice and engagement of these sacred parts of yourself to reopen to these pathways of the Divine within you.

It is not enough to think about this change. It is not enough to gather knowledge. You are tending to be unbalanced with your collecting knowledge about the world, yourself, and what is happening. It can be helpful to understand, but that will not make a difference if it is not balanced with practice and action. It is like raising a child. If you are a parent and are raising a child, it can be helpful to read books, go to classes, and talk with others about raising children. But if that is all you do, you will not serve the children. Most important is what you actually do with the children that will make a difference for them, your engagement with them every day.

Right now, you are in a grand process of transformation and growth, and you are the parent to yourself. The most important thing is your engagement, your practice with yourself on a daily basis. The Feminine parts of yourself have suffered and are shut down, atrophied, from not being embraced and engaged for so long. So now it will take practice and engagement to change that.

There are some who understand this, who have engaged this practice themselves, and who can help you to learn these practices. This one who channels this message is such a one. Now is the time to learn these practices and engage them continually. It will take time, but such a short time compared to the eons of time that these parts of you have been shut down.

Your body is beautiful. Your sexuality is sacred. Your emotions are pathways to God. Your presence is a blessed gift. Your open heart is the most powerful vessel of transformation, of receiving divine light and empowering it with love. Understand this, but do not stop there. Learn the practices for receiving and transmitting love-light through all these channels, and practice this until it becomes a dance, a joy, a beautiful part of who you are and what you bring to all.

I love you most dearly. I champion your transformation, and through that the transformation of your world.

In love and light,
I AM Mary Magdalene

*T*his was the first transmission I received from Mary. I had just begun meditating when I felt a distinct, tangible presence near me. The presence seemed especially strong around my throat, where I clearly sensed a blockage of energy. I focused my intention on releasing whatever obstructions were keeping me from opening my throat center and allowing the energy to come through. Suddenly the voice of Mary Magdalene began to speak through me, and she gave the entire message, exactly as it is written above.

After receiving her communication, I rested for a moment, glowing with the wonder and beauty of what I'd been given. My sense of peace was short-lived, however, as a disturbing thought arose in my consciousness: I probably wouldn't remember most of what she'd said! Without hesitating, I asked Mary to give me the message again while I typed it into my computer. And she did just that, repeating word for word exactly what she'd expressed the first time. If I had any remaining doubt that she had actually communicated with me, this second round of transmission totally dispelled my disbelief.

By the time she had finished, I felt infused with Mary's energy and was in a transformed state. I felt blissful, yet balanced and calm: my body was rested, my heart wide open, and my mind clear and energized. I was thrilled to have received this exquisite, powerful message. And I was amazed at her brilliance, not only in terms of the quality of her ideas but also the way she delivered her entire message in perfect form. I simply recorded her words without changing anything, and suddenly I became the custodian of impeccable insight and wisdom.

At a deeper level, I was struck by the love and compassion flowing through her words. These qualities proved to be a hallmark of all her messages: Mary didn't shy away from speaking directly about any topic, yet she voiced her ideas with kindness and care—as though shining the light of love on areas of darkness or shadow. I was amazed at the way she could address complex topics with grace and economy while still packing an enormous depth of meaning into each sentence. I came to see her style as characteristic of the way a higher-dimensional being thinks and communicates.

Mary began this communication by saying that doubt is part of our mind and that she is here to free us from it. It seems that living with chronic levels of doubt is an effect of separation from the Divine Feminine. When our minds are disconnected from the rest of ourselves—from our bodies, our sexuality, and our emotions (which Mary describes as the Feminine parts of our being)—one result is habitual doubt. I believe she wants to free us from our doubting minds through reuniting us with the Divine Feminine.

Because I have a strong tendency to doubt myself, Mary's opening statement about doubt felt personal to me. I was immediately confronted with my doubt: Was she actually communicating with me? Or was I just fabricating this whole thing? Was I evolved enough as a spiritual being to be receiving a message from Mary Magdalene? And why would she choose me?

However, as soon as she had connected with me and my feelings of doubt, she moved on to a universal message, which I sensed was what she really wanted to speak about. It was as though she was speaking to me and through me—addressing everyone who experiences doubt in any form, since the roots of doubt reside in our divorce from the Feminine parts of ourselves.

After her initial references to doubt, Mary began speaking directly about the Divine Feminine, saying she's waited two thousand years—since Yeshua's life—to bring this message. The Divine Feminine has been suppressed and denied to the point that most of us fear the Feminine and are alienated from that part of life. But now, with the "turning of the ages," the Divine Feminine is stepping forth to lead us into a new age. We are being called to love, honor, and listen to the Feminine, allowing her to lead us back into balance.

I understand the "turning of the ages" as a reference to a number of things: the transition out of the astrological age of Pisces into the age of Aquarius; the galactic alignment in 2012, which will usher in a new age of unity consciousness; and the predictions that we are on the brink of entering a new epoch in human history, which indigenous peoples sometimes refer to as the fifth world. Mary tells us that this new era is a time when the Divine Feminine can be reinstated in her rightful place as the equal partner and lover of the Divine Masculine.

Mary's emphasis on creating a foundation of understanding about the Divine Feminine was evident in her tone of calm urgency. I realized that she wants people to understand that right now is a very special time, a time that is significantly different from times past. Through her inspiring, galvanizing words I understood that she is here as an emissary of the Divine Feminine to help guide us into a new chapter in our evolution. As she clearly proclaims, the time has finally come: the Divine Feminine can now take her seat alongside the Divine Masculine. That she has been waiting two thousand years to do so is quite remarkable to me. And her reference to the Divine Feminine as partner to the Divine Masculine strongly evokes her connection with Yeshua, opening a door in my heart of great tenderness and vulnerability as I am reminded of the love bond between them that's at the core of her revelations.

Every time I return to this first message, I'm struck by Mary's power as she calls for this change. Yet, her call does not in any sense indicate a desire for the Divine Feminine to take precedence over the Divine Masculine. She's inviting us to equality, partnership, and ultimately to a union of the two. The Divine Masculine has been deprived of his partner for a very long time, and at last the partnership with her can be reestablished. This union isn't just "out there" somewhere, outside of us. Mary emphasizes that this same partnership lives within each of us. Thus, she's simultaneously calling us to partnership in the external world and to our wholeness as individually manifest beings.

Mary devotes the rest of the message to showing what reconnecting with the Divine Feminine will mean. She begins by making a distinction between our lower mind and our sacred mind.

The lower mind is the part of the mind that generates our usual, everyday thinking. It has two parts: the subconscious and the rational. The subconscious mind is the domain of instinct, sensory information, emotional-sexual drives and feelings, discernment of differences and similarities, memory, and beliefs. The rational mind retains and recalls information; comprehends; applies learned material to new situations; analyzes experience to gain understanding; combines concepts to form new ideas; and creates, which involves drawing on all of the other rational functions and also incorporating value judgments to produce something new. The rational mind generates many of the mental processes we associate with thinking, such as forming conclusions, generalizing, projecting from one situation to another, decision making, problem solving, thinking about the future, and learning from our experience.

Figure 1-1. SACRED MIND AND HEART—LOWER MIND

SACRED MIND
Inspiration, presence, awareness, insight, creativity, connection to collective consciousness, psychic powers

SACRED HEART
Love, compassion, blessing, forgiveness

LOWER MIND
Rational Mind: Knowledge, comprehension, application, analysis, synthesis, creation

Subconscious Mind: Instinct, sensation, emotional/sexual drives and feelings, discernment of differences and similarities, memory, beliefs

Obviously, the functions of our lower mind are essential; it's when they start to overrule the heart that they become problematic. To say this in a more positive way, Mary is urging us to use our thinking mind in service to our feeling heart. What is our feeling heart? I regard *feelings* as including both our emotions and our visceral sensations, and the heart as the center of our Feminine manifestation of Divinity, expressing the qualities of love, compassion, forgiveness, and blessing. Thus, the feeling heart integrates our feeling capacity as incarnate beings with the Feminine aspect of our God-nature.

I observe two common tendencies relative to feelings and the heart. One is to be connected to emotions and sensory input but less connected to the heart qualities of love, compassion, forgiveness, and blessing. People who have this tendency are sometimes perceived as overly dramatic. The opposite inclination is to be connected to the heart qualities of love, compassion, blessing, and forgiveness but not as connected to the emotions and the senses. People with this tendency may be viewed as "airy-fairy." Mary shows us how to integrate these partial ways of relating to our experience. As in so many instances, she directs us to balance through union—in this case, the union of feelings and the heart.

Mary recommends that we allow the feeling heart and lower mind to work together, with the feeling heart taking precedence. You might picture the lower mind as a team of loyal advisors to a leader. Each counselor provides valuable input from a particular focus, which may represent a narrow point of view. The feeling heart is the head of state that integrates all these perspectives with wisdom and then sets the course of action for all.

We often reverse this process and allow the lower mind to rule the heart. For a simple example, many people, when asked whether they would like something to eat, habitually respond by checking to see what time it is. Although we frequently decide when to eat based on the time of day, we're really designed to feed ourselves when we *feel hungry* as opposed to when our rational minds tell us that it's time to refuel. (Of course, there are exceptions, such as certain medical conditions that require us to eat even if we're not hungry, but I'm sure you get the idea.) Eating by the clock can lead to problems such as overeating, since we don't necessarily need food just because we tell ourselves it's "time to eat." Perhaps even more significant, it can contribute to a sense of disconnection from the natural world, in which we relate to our bodies as machines that regularly get serviced. The feeling heart, on the other hand, experiences the body's natural rhythms and cycles, its internal communication of appetite, and the pleasure of eating when we're truly hungry, and it trusts that we will be guided to well-being through listening to our bodies.

In addition to aligning our rational mind with our feeling heart, Mary says we need to develop the ability to surrender our thinking to pure presence, which is one of the functions of our sacred, or higher, mind. When we meditate, we connect to pure presence, experiencing it as a state of stillness, peace, tranquility, spaciousness, and timelessness, in which we're totally present to what *is*. You might think of it is as the presence of God.

The sacred mind is the seat of the Divine Masculine within individually manifest beings and is most often associated with the pineal gland in the center of the head. Its other functions include inspiration, awareness, insight, creativity, connection to the collective consciousness, and psychic powers.

To summarize, Mary is advocating two things in her first message: that we use our lower minds in service to our feeling heart and that we develop the ability to surrender our thinking to pure presence.

Mary goes on to say that when we have accomplished these two things, the veils surrounding the sacred mind can be lifted, allowing the marriage of the sacred heart and sacred mind to occur. I find this depiction exceedingly beautiful and inspiring. I picture a bride, lifting her veil to meet the eyes of her beloved. I believe Mary intended this as a literal description of a real process. I hear her telling us that veils cover the sacred mind, which is why we don't automatically know or experience it. It's also why we need to engage in spiritual practices if we want to grow and change: it takes intention and practice to lift these veils.

Many teachings explain how to quiet our minds and surrender to pure presence through meditation, but Mary focuses on a less-discussed practice: strengthening the feeling heart through opening to the Feminine parts of ourselves. This strengthening will allow a natural rebalancing to occur, in which the lower mind can calm down and function in service to the heart. And she gives us a glimpse of where these capacities will lead us, saying that the veils will lift and a marriage will occur between our inner Masculine (through the sacred mind) and our inner Feminine (through the sacred heart).

One of my spiritual teachers, Adi Da, particularly exemplified this internal sacred marriage of the Masculine and Feminine. Those who heard him were riveted by his delightful wit and penetrating insights. Yet, what stood out even more was the force of love and blessing that I and so many others felt in his presence. People regularly fell into sobs of joy and gratitude in response to the opening of the heart they experienced through their contact with him. I've heard similar descriptions from many people who've interacted with an advanced spiritual being.

When the sacred heart and sacred mind are in union, Mary instructs us to bring light into our bodies, merge it with love, and send the empowered love-light out into the world. I believe she's referring to both a state and an ongoing process of merging light and love within us and then radiating it out into the world. Mary calls the receiving and transmission of love-light in this way "a celebration of ongoing joy." Clearly, it is also a powerful vehicle for transforming us and our world.

A simple version of the inner union of light and love involves drawing unconditional love up into the lower chakras and the heart. This is the love of the Divine Feminine, which we may visualize as emanating from the earth. We draw this love up through the soles of our feet or the base of our spine and into the heart.

Once this is established, we continue drawing love into the heart as we begin to draw Creator-Light down into our sacred mind and heart. This is the light of the Divine Masculine, which we can visualize as coming from the sun, the heavens, or the great central sun of the universe. The light enters through the crown of the head, which is the gateway to our higher self, to the higher dimensions, and ultimately to the Supreme Creator. From there, we draw the light down into the sacred mind and then into the heart, where it merges with the love.

In that merging, love-light becomes activated and empowered so that it can be sent out to the rest of our body and the world. You can coordinate this process with the breath, drawing love and light into the heart with the inhalation, merging the two, and then, with the exhalation, sending out activated love-light.

Mary closes her message by reminding us that thinking alone is not sufficient for us to progress and evolve. Practice and engagement are required. Her admonition points to another symptom of imbalance between the Masculine and Feminine—the tendency to focus on thinking rather than on applying our body and energy toward what we desire.

Mary repeatedly observes that we have ignored the building blocks that form the foundation of our inner Divine Feminine and support our feeling heart. In other words, we have ignored our bodies, our sexuality, and our feelings. She calls us to value, love, and fully incarnate these parts of ourselves so that we can come into balance with the Masculine. Reestablishing this balance provides a necessary platform for our spiritual growth, freedom, and happiness, and she tells us very specifically how to do it.

In all of Mary's communications, I felt her beckoning to me and to all people to take in her ideas and let them transform us. Not only that, I strongly felt her blessing everyone to *experience* a taste of her

Figure 1-2. BREATHING LOVE AND LIGHT

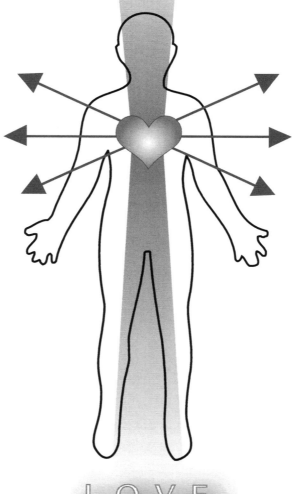

On inhaled breath, draw in love and light.

On exhaled breath, send out love-light.

reality. As I received these communications, I was drawn into the magnificence of her vision:

> Your body is beautiful. Your sexuality is sacred. Your emotions are pathways to God. Your presence is a blessed gift. Your open heart is the most powerful vessel of transformation, of receiving divine light and empowering it with love.... Learn the practices for receiving and transmitting love-light through all these channels, and practice this until it becomes a dance, a joy, a beautiful part of who you are and what you bring to all.

Mary's words ignited my desire to realize the state she describes and filled me with confidence that it is fully within my reach. I felt her laying out the path before me so I can walk from where I am now to the beauty of which she speaks. This awe-inspiring gift is one that is still alive inside me and is renewed each time I read her communications. For this, I feel tremendous gratitude and excitement. My sincere hope is that by sharing these messages with you, along with my understandings and experiences, you, too, will be drawn into Mary's world of divine union. So may it be!

TWO

Loving Your Body, Sexuality, and Emotions

Dear one ~

It is so easy to get distracted, especially by your mind. It is essential to learn to quiet your mind. And this must be supported. The computer is one way that you can become addicted to a mind-based reality.

You must fall in love again with your body, your feelings, your emotions, your heart—and all this must be directed by a loving will. This is the platform or foundation for opening to the higher realms of beauty and light that you so long for. I call you to this and assure you that it is worth it. It is so beautiful and joyful here. And in this place, you will unite with your sacred mind, your beloved partner in wholeness, which is what is mirrored and reflected in your lower mind but never satisfied there.

It is good that you have developed your mind. What you suffer is that you have not developed the other parts of your lower being in balance, and so you are out of balance. Now, you have become used to a mind-dominated existence. So you require rebalancing in order to continue on your path of growth and opening. That rebalancing involves quieting the mind, being able to set it aside at will, by choice, and also using it by choice, just as you use your legs by choice. If your legs were always moving and going, it would interfere with your life. So it is with your mind.

It is not enough to only quiet your mind. You must also strengthen and grow the other parts of yourself that are needed for wholeness. There is the physical body. There is already a great deal of information and help available relative to becoming healthy in the physical body—eating well, exercising, healing illnesses, and so on. The parts that many of you now need are two things. Both are about loving your bodies.

The first is to relate to your body as a sacred temple, a beautiful manifestation of God. This is difficult for many of you who have shame about your body, feel that something is wrong with your body, or feel that it's ugly or sinful or just not right. You don't feel this way about a flower. You don't feel this way about a pet. You probably don't feel this way about your friends. So you must learn to love your body. Look at it with love. This can be done in front of a mirror, as an actual practice. You can touch your body with love. Perhaps there are places on your body that you've learned not to touch, and they are beautiful and sacred, too. Touch your whole body with love. Can you feel it coming to life?

You are a sacred healer as you transmit love, and you can heal your shame and your separateness from your self and your own body with love. Through bringing your love to your body, you release the blocks and negative messages and once again let your light shine through your physical form. True beauty is of the light. It's not about the composition of the form. The form is a medium for conducting light.

The other area of your physical that needs to be brought forward is your sexuality. This is an area that very few people in the spiritual world are speaking about, but it is so important because it, too, is sacred. Through sexuality, you have the power to bring forth new life. What could be more sacred than that?

There are two ways you can bring forth new life. One is through procreation—conceiving and birthing a child. The other is through giving birth to your spiritual self. These are the two true functions of sexuality. If you are not engaging sexuality for these purposes, it tends to become a trap or even an addiction to tension-release with a brief glimpse of union, connection, and ecstasy. That union is really union with the Divine, and that is the true function of sexuality. You can learn to consciously and intentionally make your sexuality about that. Then it is a form of communion with the Divine and will open you to your higher self and the higher realms, rather than discharge your energy downward and outward.

There are teachings and practices for engaging sexuality in this way. Some call it sacred sexuality. In the Egyptian lineage that I came from, it was known as the Sex Magic of Isis or the Alchemy of Horus, depending on whether it was practiced with a partner or solo. In the Indian tradition, it is known as Tantra or kundalini yoga. There are people today, including this woman who I am communicating through, who know these practices and can teach them to others.

Very closely tied to the physical body is the emotional body. Much maligning has been done in relationship to the emotional body. You might say that it's gotten a lot of "bad press." That is because there is great power in the emotions. Many have taught you to deny and suppress your emotions because, then, you are cut off from your power and are easy to control. It is essential that you reconnect with your emotions and feelings, because these are essential pathways of connection to your heart.

Emotions are a particularly human function. Many beings are highly developed in their mental powers, but emotions are a human gift. It is your strength, and even your calling as part of the universal plan, to be leaders in the emotional realm. Humans are still coming up to this calling and learning how to embrace and make use of the power of emotions.

The key to emotions is to fully feel them. Most of you have been trained to be afraid of your emotions and to stave them off. This is the opposite of what will set you free and maintain your power. Feeling your emotions does not mean reacting to them or acting upon them. It means opening fully to them. It's like a woman receiving her lover. It's about receiving them and fully being with them. Perhaps you might think of a mother holding a crying child, not trying to talk to the child or fix the problem, but just holding the child and feeling with the child, helping the child to center and be with the pain. The feelings themselves lead us to the healing we require and through to the other side. We can trust that process.

Emotions are always motivated by beautiful qualities, what I would call divine aspects of ourselves. By letting ourselves fully feel and experience our emotions, we will be led to these divine aspects. Then we will be ready to act because, then, our actions will come from our higher self.

Some of what you call emotions or feelings are not pure feeling states. They are mixed with judgmental thoughts of right and wrong. These include anger, depression, guilt, shame, abandonment, betrayal, and many others. So part of the learning is to discern true feelings from judgments and thoughts. In that discernment, the judgmental thinking dissolves and leads to the true feeling that the judgmental thinking was masking.

These three areas—loving your body, embracing sexuality and sexual energy for uniting with and birthing your divine self, and treasuring and uniting with your feelings to lead you to Source—all three of these are vital for creating the foundation of wholeness, which will open the doorways to your spiritual growth in the higher realms. And so I call you to embrace these with wisdom and love, and this will transform you, and even will transform all of humanity.

These are the doorways to the future, the keys to opening the passage into a glorious future. These are the mechanics of embodying and embracing the Divine Feminine, which is coming to the fore to lead us into a beautiful future of union with the Feminine and Masculine, just as our Father-Mother God abides in union. As above, so below.

I love you and support you in this wonderful transformation.
I AM Mary Magdalene

*M*ary begins this talk by telling us we need to learn how to quiet our lower minds, which have become overactive and dominant. We need to fall in love again with our bodies, our sexuality, our emotions, and our hearts. Many of us have become so alienated from these parts of ourselves that we live in our thoughts rather than in our bodies, and we repress our sexuality and emotions. To get a sense of how out of balance we are, visualize an old-fashioned scale with two plates, one on each side. One side holds the mind, and the other side holds the body, sexuality, and emotions. The mind side is so heavy that it rests on the ground, and the body side so light that it dangles far up in the sky. We need to bring these two parts of ourselves back into balance

Mary alludes to our mind-based reality (which is supported by our dependence on computers and other electronic devices) as the source of our imbalance. Even our spirituality, with its focus on mental techniques such as calming our thoughts and creating what we want through the mind, tends to be mind-dominated. In fact, mastering the mind is part of the equation. We need to be able to still the mind and set our thoughts aside at will. But mental control alone is not sufficient. In order to continue on our path of spiritual growth and opening, we have to rebalance our minds and hearts. This requires strengthening the parts of ourselves we've become cut off from: our bodies, our sexuality, and our emotions. In this message, Mary begins to give specific instructions for how to do this.

First, she provides a vision of what will happen when we open to our bodies, emotions, and hearts. This opening will lead us into higher realms of light, where we'll experience joy and beauty. Here, we'll be able to unite with our sacred mind, which she refers to as "your beloved partner in wholeness." We'll enjoy the qualities of the sacred mind: inspiration, presence, awareness, insight, creativity, connection to the collective consciousness, and psychic powers. Our lower mind mirrors our sacred mind, but because it's only a reflection of our higher faculties, we don't find the satisfaction we seek there. Satisfaction comes through reunion with our sacred mind, which will happen once we create equilibrium between our lower mind and heart.

Turning her attention to practical steps for achieving this balance, Mary emphasizes the importance of loving our bodies. Much wisdom already exists about certain aspects of loving our bodies, such as eating a healthy diet, exercising, and healing illness or dis-ease. Here, Mary focuses on two areas that aren't so commonly discussed: our feeling relationship with our physical bodies and our sexuality. Using a metaphor rich with guidance about living in right relationship with our bodies, she instructs us to relate to our bodies as sacred temples.

Imagine the Taj Mahal. Picture yourself loving and caring for your body as devotedly as that sacred temple is served. Feel the peace and serenity of the temple, and imagine experiencing the same peace and centeredness in your body.

Are you at peace with your body? Do you feel love and appreciation for it? Do you enjoy it? Do you relate to it as a manifestation of divinity? Can you love your body in the same way that you love a flower? Can you accept your body the way you accept the body of a pet or favorite animal? Can you see your body as beautiful in the way you see your friends as beautiful? If you're not able to wholeheartedly answer yes to all these questions, you're most likely holding some degree of shame about your body. This shame manifests as a sense that there's something wrong with your body: that it's tainted or evil, unattractive, too fat, too thin, too old, damaged, or somehow not right or good enough.

Mary suggests a simple practice for healing shame about our bodies. She tells us to look at and touch our bodies with love. We can heal our bodies through loving touch, which is similar to the way energy-healers work, or even to the way that Yeshua healed people.

For many of us, the suggestion of looking at and touching our bodies is likely to provoke negative reactions: thoughts that we *shouldn't* do that, or thoughts that it's silly or a waste of time or not necessary. We may experience a whole range of feelings while looking at our bodies or touching them with love, including feelings of shame or repulsion. We may feel guilty, as if we're doing something wrong or bad or sinful; this guilt may be connected with judgments about being self-absorbed, self-centered, conceited, vain, or licentious. We may experience feelings of sadness and mourning for how distant we feel from our bodies. Opening to these or any other feelings that arise is essential to healing our disconnection from our physical selves. Mary's instruction about embracing our feelings and fully being with them applies to all the emotions this exercise evokes.

The second area of loving our bodies involves loving our sexuality. Most of us carry deep scars in our psyches from negative religious, spiritual, and cultural messages against sexuality. Mary herself was virtually banished from the religious accounts of Jesus's life because of her associations with sexuality and the body. In this respect, she serves as a symbol for all women and for the Feminine in general, for the Feminine has been largely eliminated from most traditions of religion and spirituality. But the time is ripe for this to change. Now, the Feminine is to be honored and loved and valued alongside the Masculine. A central part of this change involves valuing and loving our sexuality.

Honoring our sexuality doesn't mean that we suddenly start to engage in sexual orgies. That's the kind of reaction that occurs when part of us has been suppressed and is finally released. Repressed energy is like a volcano exploding, releasing the long pent-up pressure of containment. Ironically, many people experience this kind of release during sex. Mary refers to this type of sexuality as "tension-release," and it is how most people have learned to engage in sex.

Both the tension of suppression and the tension-release that follows are simply two manifestations within the same cycle. One naturally leads to the other. Mary calls us to a whole different kind of intimacy: sexuality as a form of communion with the Divine. If our bodies are sacred temples of the Divine, then our sexuality becomes one of the sacraments of the temple. She points to traditions that teach sacred sexuality, including the Egyptian tradition from the temples of Isis and the Indian tradition of Tantra. Today, we can learn these sacred forms of sexuality from individuals who are contemporary teachers of these arts so that we can engage our sexual energy for its highest purposes, which are communing with the Divine and giving birth to our divine selves.

When we've fully embraced our sexuality as beautiful and integral to our nature, we'll have as natural a relationship to sexuality as we do to food. Imagine returning from a vacation and telling your friends and family about the delicious food you relished on your trip. Now imagine telling an open-minded friend about the ecstatic sexual experiences you delighted in. If you don't feel the same level of comfort and ease in the second conversation, you probably have some work to do in loving your sexuality.

In the rest of her message, Mary focuses on one of her main themes: our relationship to our feelings. Connecting to our feelings is critical, she explains, because it makes us powerful; conversely, when we're disconnected from our feelings, we're easy to control.

I remember the first time I participated in a consensus-based group. I felt concern that I wouldn't be happy with the decisions the group made. A friend responded to my worry by telling me, "Just don't agree to anything you don't feel good about." While this assuaged my anxiety, I discovered that it wasn't easy for me to do. I watched myself consent to things I didn't feel a wholehearted yes to, and later I felt dissatisfied with my choices. I realized I had strong habits of complying with others, especially when I judged them to be more powerful than I. Because of my tendency to discount my feelings, staying in my power by sticking with my feelings proved to be quite challenging.

The idea that our feelings make us powerful is supported by the principles of manifestation. Many teachings on how to create what we want in our lives assert that feelings are the fuel that drives our ability to manifest. When we disconnect from our feelings, we're actually disconnecting from our power of manifestation. A robot is the ultimate example of living without feelings, and robots are specifically created to be controlled by others.

Yet, feelings serve an even more important function than connecting us to our power. Feelings are the pathway to our hearts. For many of us, however, this pathway is obstructed. We've been trained to direct our energy away from our feelings and into judgmental thinking by condemning someone or something as wrong. This conditioning keeps us from communicating with our hearts. Small children, before they're indoctrinated in "right" and "wrong," simply experience their feelings with no judgments about anyone or anything being wrong. This is the acceptance and embrace of our feelings that Mary advocates.

Many of us perceive ourselves as strong when we're in a position of judging others, but, really, the opposite is true. We abandon our power and our freedom when we choose judging over feeling. Our strength comes from our feeling hearts, not from our critical minds. For example, if you have declared that something is a bad idea, you've made yourself vulnerable to someone arguing that it's a good idea out of a need to prove you wrong. On the other hand, if you were to say instead that you felt uncomfortable with the idea, you would be in a strong position because feelings simply are not arguable. We are our own authority on what we feel, and we remain in a position of innate potency when we stay connected to our feeling hearts.

Mary sees our unique role in the universe as centered on emotions: while many other beings have highly developed mental abilities, our uniqueness and strength as humans lies in our capacity to be emotional. In fact, we are called to be leaders in the emotional realm, a role we're still growing into. By showing us how to embrace our emotions and make use of their power, Mary is helping us to fulfill our part in the universal design.

The key to actualizing our potential for emotional mastery is to fully feel our emotions, which is different from either repressing them or reacting to them. It's about opening to our emotions, like a woman receiving her lover, as Mary says. It's about receiving our feelings and being with them fully. She suggests the image of a mother holding a crying child and not trying to distract the child or talk the child out of the feelings. We can simply be present to our feelings while providing a sense of safety and support in which we can feel them fully.

If we learn to accept our emotions, we'll be led to the true source of our feelings, which Mary describes as divine aspects of ourselves. In reality, our feelings are indicators of our longing for these beautiful parts of ourselves. I think of feelings as similar to the warning lights on an automobile dashboard. They provide information about what's going on with the engine. If we kept a hammer in the car and smashed the signal when the red light came on, we'd be preventing the warning device from doing its job. What is more, we'd probably suffer the results of ignoring the engine's service requirements. Denying or suppressing our feelings does the same thing: it keeps us from attending to the divine qualities within ourselves that need our attention. When we open to our feelings, they can serve their natural function, which is to lead us to these beautiful qualities.

Here's an example of how this works in life. Let's say I had plans to go to the movies with a friend, who called at the last minute and told me she had changed her mind. I might feel disappointed and sad. I could use those feelings to judge my friend. I could convince myself that she'd done something wrong and criticize her for being unreliable. Or I could judge myself and tell myself that I shouldn't feel upset and that it's no big deal. Those are the kinds of responses most of us have learned. We distract ourselves from our emotions by turning our energy outward and blaming the other person or by turning the energy inward and judging ourselves.

Mary proposes a different path. She suggests we open up to our feelings and let ourselves fully experience the disappointment or sadness or whatever it is we're feeling. Doing this allows our emotions to lead us to their true source—something beautiful within that we've been longing for. In this example, the desired beautiful quality or divine aspect might be companionship and connection.

When I connect with the source of my feelings—in this case, my desire for companionship and connection—a shift happens in me.

The emotions I'm experiencing—disappointment and sadness—dissipate as I become more connected to the inner qualities of companionship and connection, which I experience as they exist in me in their fullness. In other words, I can connect with the fulfilled state of companionship or connection within myself, and in so doing, I reconnect with the Divine. I shift from a sense of deficiency based on outer circumstances to a sense of wholeness whose source is in the always-already-full nature of my inner divine aspects. Through this, I am returned to peace.

Once I'm rested in my wholeness, I can move into action. I may ask another friend to go with me to the movie, I may go by myself, or I may find something else to do and make plans with my friend for another night. The choices I have are as limitless as my creativity. What's important is that now I'm acting out of the wholeness and peace that come from already being connected to the Divine, rather than reacting to a sense of being cut off due to external events.

The teaching of Nonviolent Communication lists the beautiful qualities that are at the root of our feelings and calls these qualities "needs." I consider these needs to be equivalent to what Mary describes as our "inner divine qualities," or aspects. Figure 2-1 provides a list of these source qualities to help us become familiar with them. You can also use the list to help you identify the specific aspects of divinity that are calling to you in any moment.

Mary points out that some of the states we often call feelings are actually not pure feelings. Anger, depression, shame, and guilt—which are mixed with negative judgments—all fall within this category. Also, we often refer to the behaviors of *others*, such as abandonment or betrayal, as feelings, but they are really actions rather than feelings, and they are usually mixed with judgments of right and wrong. For example, if you have the thought that someone has abandoned you, the pure feeling beneath that thought might be

Figure 2-1. LIST OF INNER DIVINE QUALITIES

The chart below comes from the Center for Nonviolent Communication.
It is an excellent list of our inner divine qualities, which are the source of our feelings.

Needs Inventory

The following list of needs is neither exhaustive nor definitive. It is meant as a starting place to support anyone who wishes to engage in a process of deepening self-discovery and to facilitate greater understanding and connection between people.

CONNECTION

acceptance
affection
appreciation
belonging
cooperation
communication
closeness
community
companionship
compassion
consideration
consistency
empathy
inclusion
intimacy
love
mutuality
nurturing
respect/self-respect
safety
security
stability
support
to know and be known
to see and be seen
to understand and be
understood
trust
warmth

PHYSICAL WELL-BEING

air
food
movement/exercise
rest/sleep
sexual expression
safety
shelter
touch
water

HONESTY

authenticity
integrity
presence

PLAY

joy
humor

PEACE

beauty
communion
ease
equality
harmony
inspiration
order

MEANING

awareness
celebration of life
challenge
clarity
competence
consciousness
contribution
creativity
discovery
efficacy
effectiveness
growth
hope
learning
mourning
participation
purpose
self-expression
stimulation
to matter
understanding

AUTONOMY

choice
freedom
independence
space
spontaneity

sadness, loneliness, fear, disappointment, or even relief. Mary instructs us to use our powers of discernment to separate our judgments of wrong or right from the actual feeling. At that point, we will be able to engage the practice she recommends in regard to the pure feeling.

I feel deeply grateful for Mary's instruction about balancing the mind with the body and feelings. So often we get trapped in mental spirals because we're locked into habits of judgmental thinking. Mary clarifies a practical pathway out of that prison and leads us into the peace and harmony of connection with the Divine.

Mary closes with her vision of the union of the Masculine and Feminine. These are my favorite parts of her messages because I can glimpse the marvel and glory of union with the Divine as she experiences it and feel the magnitude of her unconditional love. When I was receiving the closing of her messages, I felt infused with her love. I felt her supporting me to live the experience with her in that moment. And each time I reread the messages even now, I experience that again.

And so I end my commentary with Mary's closing, which so moves me:

> These are the doorways to the future, the keys to opening the passage into a glorious future. These are the mechanics of embodying and embracing the Divine Feminine, which is coming to the fore to lead us into a beautiful future of union with the Feminine and Masculine, just as our Father-Mother God abides in union. As above, so below. I love you and support you in this wonderful transformation.

THREE

Responding to Pain

Dear one ~

Today I will talk to you of pain. It is something I know much about. Many of you are very confused about pain and how to respond to it. You're even confused about why there is pain. So I would like to clarify this.

Your pain is given to you to help you grow. Do you believe this? It is a difficult medicine. The pain is actually the medicine. When you have pain, it is telling you that there is some way that you have closed off from God. If you only seek to make the pain go away, then you will not receive the help you are being given for you to change, heal, and grow. Most of your responses to pain are about making it go away—taking a medicine or drug, numbing yourself with distractions, diverting yourself by blaming others or some situation, or trying to "fix" it so that you don't have to feel the pain.

It's not that you have to stay in the pain. But if you just try to get rid of the pain, you won't receive the benefit. So there is another way.

When you are in pain, you must turn to God. That is, for many of you, a hard thing to do. You think that the pain is proof that God has deserted you. In fact, God is calling to you through the pain. God loves you and wants to help you, and pain is one avenue.

45

So, when you feel pain, turn to God. You may need a spiritual friend to help you in that moment if it is too hard for you to turn in the midst of pain. It is a good time to call on your strongest spiritual friend who will help you turn to God.

However you do it, through prayer or asking for help from another or meditating, turn to God first. Ask God to help you. Ask all your angels, Spirit helpers, and beings of light you're connected to, to help you. Ask them to work with the situation. Ask them to connect with the Christ consciousness of the other people involved and to help you connect with Christ consciousness. Ask your Spirit helpers to connect with the Spirit helpers of any other beings involved. Ask for the highest outcome for all involved. Ask that, "Thy will be done," which is a way of inviting the highest beings to be involved for the good of all. Ask that Christ consciousness be infused into the situation and that it alter the events in whatever way is for the best for all. Ask until you feel yourself let go. That is surrender. You will know it because you come to peace.

Ask to be guided as to what you should do. Then your actions will come from your connection to Christ consciousness, from your surrender and peace. You may do things you would never have thought of otherwise because your creativity has been opened up through your connection to Source. You are being infused with higher ideas. You might be guided to do what you would have done before you turned to God, but you will be doing it from a different place, from a place of peace and surrender.

Do this as often as you need to when you are in pain—physical pain or emotional pain. You might feel the surrender and peace for a while and then slip back into your old way of thinking—fearing the pain and worrying about what's going to happen, perhaps feeling angry about what you think are the causes of the pain, maybe even angry about life or angry at God. "It's not fair. Why me? What did I do to deserve this?" And so on. All of that is a sign that you've slipped back into your little mind, where you're not connected to God. Then you need to take another step: go back to prayer, to meditation, to asking for help from someone stronger in that moment, to asking for help from God.

Asking is so important. We respect your free will. Even though we want to help you, we will not step in until you ask. We ask the same of you with others. Respect their free will. This can be difficult if you perceive that they are in pain and you want to help them. Or perhaps you judge that they're doing things wrong, that they *should* be doing things differently, and that you *should* correct them or step in and change things for them, tell them what to do. You do not know what the divine plan for them is. You might be interfering with a grand opportunity that they are receiving. It is essential that you respect their free choice.

Of course, if you are a parent, you are in a position of making decisions for your children, but only to the point that they are not capable. It is very important that you be aware of what they are capable of deciding and respect their choices in these arenas. As they grow, allow them to participate more and more in making choices with you, guiding them in learning how to make choices that are for the best for all. And as you see them capable of making their own choices, allow them to do so.

Free choice is a divine attribute that you on Earth have been given, and respecting it is part of being aligned to the Divine. If you think someone is hurting you or someone else, first turn to prayer, asking the beings of light to shift the scenario for the highest good of all. Ask them to work with the beings of light that are connected to all involved. Ask them to guide you and everyone else to be in alignment with Christ consciousness. When your heart is open and you have come to peace, then you can wait to receive guidance on what you should do. You will know it is guidance if it sustains your peace and keeps your heart open.

You are not alone. You are never alone. This is the greatest challenge for human beings to learn. It is the challenge of having been born as a seemingly separate individual. We are here with you always. Just call upon us, and we are here. We are powerful and we are for your highest good.

I love you, and my heart is with you.
I AM Mary Magdalene

*M*ary offers us so much in this transmission. She begins by sharing that she knows a lot about pain and then presents her point of view about it: pain is given to help us grow. It's actually a form of medicine that she compassionately refers to as "difficult medicine." On one hand, pain is a signal that we've closed off from God in some way. But it's more than just an indication of disconnection. Pain is really a call to turn toward God, reconnect with God, and receive God's guidance. We could see it as God extending a hand to us. When we respond to pain with this attitude, pain becomes our ally in helping us to become whole again.

Mary's perspective stands in contrast to the way most of us react to pain. In general, we don't see pain as a gift and choose to embrace it; on the contrary, our usual response is to try and get away from it. Our reactions to pain seem to be hardwired into our system as primal survival mechanisms. We try to numb pain—with painkillers and positive thoughts and even by denying that we're in pain. And we distract ourselves with activities. We may try to escape our feelings by projecting hurt outward onto others: blaming, criticizing, or even physically abusing (the kick-the-dog-when-we-feel-hurt syndrome). We may turn our hurt inward, blaming and criticizing ourselves. Or we may keep busy by analyzing the cause of the pain and trying to fix it or make it go away.

Typically, we use a combination of these strategies, trying to make pain disappear as quickly as possible. Mary asks us to consider a different approach: rather than trying to get away from pain, we can use it to turn to God.

I don't hear Mary judging us in any way, either for having pain or for our tendency to try to avoid it. She is not saying that we're bad, wrong, evil, or sinful because we have pain. She is not pointing to pain as evidence that we're somehow spiritually lost, less-than, or in any way wrong. And she is not belittling anyone for the tendency to avoid pain. She simply states what she observes and suggests another way of viewing and responding to pain, giving us a more helpful perspective than our characteristic responses. She wants to help us and has no need to make us wrong or inferior.

Mary's nonjudgmental attitude is quite different from the messages so many of us have received and internalized from various religious and spiritual teachings. For example, there's a Puritan belief that is still influencing many people, consciously or subconsciously. It points to what happens in our lives as evidence of our spiritual correctness or lack thereof. Thus, if we're in pain, it's a sign that we've sinned or done something wrong. In other words, pain is seen as a form of punishment from God for our errors or as a necessary penance to cleanse us of wrongdoing.

A similar kind of thinking can occur with the more contemporary belief that we create our reality. This concept can be interpreted to mean that if we're in pain, it's a sign of unconsciousness or failure on our part to manifest a perfect life. For example, I've heard people respond to someone who is expressing that they're having difficulties by asking, "How have you created this situation?" While I believe there is value in considering that question, it all too often carries with it a subtle judgment that the individual *should* have created something more positive, and if they're having a hard time, it must be their fault.

By contrast, Mary simply describes the ways that many of us tend to operate—without judging or blaming us—and suggests a different option. She remains completely loving while still seeing other possibilities that are more supportive of our growth and well-being. Rather than avoiding pain or beating ourselves up because we're in pain, she suggests we use it as a call to turn to God.

Although Mary doesn't condemn pain, she also recognizes it as a hardship. She's not saying that we should just accept the pain and live with it. She's not calling on us to be martyrs and do nothing. She's asking us to understand pain in a new way, as a message from God to come home. Mary tells us not to miss the gift and the opportunity. Rather than focusing immediately on getting out of pain, turn to God. Reconnect with God. Come to peace in God. And let God direct your actions.

For most of us, this response isn't easy or natural. It certainly isn't for me. To support us, Mary gives specific steps to follow, clarifying that these steps apply to both physical and emotional pain. We can pray, turning to God and asking for God's help. We can meditate, allowing ourselves to become quiet and receptive to God. We can enlist the help of spiritually aware friends, who can help us open to God in the midst of pain and help us notice what happens when we do that. We can call on angels, Spirit guides, or beings of light, and we can ask our Spirit guides or angels to work with the Spirit guides or angels of others involved. We can call on Christ consciousness for ourselves and others. These are all ways of asking God for help.

Since Mary uses the term *Christ consciousness* a number of

times in this message, I'd like to clarify what it means. I view Christ consciousness as the consciousness that Yeshua embodied and from which he acted. It's the consciousness of God, manifesting in humans. Some people refer to Christ consciousness as the I AM presence or the indwelling Divine. The literal meaning of the word *Christ* is "anointed." Thus, I understand Christ consciousness to refer to being anointed with the consciousness of God. The reference to anointment also evokes, for me, images of Mary anointing Yeshua out of her love for him and her devotion to the consciousness that he embodied.

Mary instructs us to keep asking for God's help in whatever way seems right for us until we feel ourselves let go. This is a shift we can clearly feel: we'll know we've let go because we'll experience peace. When we are resisting pain, we may think that we are directing our energy toward escaping it, but, actually, we are holding onto it. It's not until we open to God that we let go. We allow God to take charge. In that surrender, we come to peace.

While writing this book, I experienced my own personal struggle with holding on and refusing to surrender. I had decided I wanted the book to come out by November 11, 2011 (11/11/11), partly because I believed that was the time frame Mary wanted and partly because I thought it would be an auspicious date to release the book. As the deadline drew nearer, I started to feel crunched because I had more to do than seemed possible within the allotted time. I buckled down to work, telling myself I could finish the book if I just stayed disciplined and made optimum use of every moment. I began cutting back on everything in my life that wasn't essential for completing the book and became increasingly serious and driven to meet the goal. Finally, a friend came over to visit and was shocked to see the state of stress I was in. I admitted I'd become so frazzled that I wasn't even getting much done on the book.

My friend helped me to see that I was operating out of "creature power," thinking that I could muscle my way through to create what I had in mind. He helped guide me to a whole new path of letting go of my plan and allowing God to take over. I was so attached to the date I'd chosen that it wasn't easy for me to release my cling-ing—even though it looked as if it might kill me if I continued push-ing myself. Yet, with my friend's loving encouragement, I was able to surrender my agenda and invite God to take charge. In doing so, I did indeed come to peace.

Once we reach that place of peace, we can receive guidance from God about how to act. Often this guidance helps us act from the heart rather than from reactivity. When we become sensitive, we can feel the difference between these two. God's guidance can also open us to seeing new, creative possibilities that previously weren't available. We're guided on how to care for ourselves, as well as on how to relate to others who are involved in the situation.

In my case, I was clearly directed to bring my life back into bal-ance by taking time to eat well, exercise, see friends, have fun, and nurture myself. I began to follow my heart's true guidance instead of the frenzied, self-destructive program I'd created to meet my goal. Once I began taking care of myself, the writing started flowing again and I saw that what was emerging was much stronger than before. I realized that the book had its own birthing process, with its own timing. My ludicrous attempt to dictate the timetable had clearly been counterproductive. Happily, I watched as the book resumed its natural unfoldment.

Allowing God to guide us like this opens us to a state of grace. We experience deep peace in which we *know* that we're not alone or separate and that, at a deeper level, all is in divine order. Mary suggests pain can be a potent doorway into this state of grace. Ap-proached as a way to God, our experience of pain can be very different from what it is when we see it as the enemy. It's also true that we may slip from this state of grace, sliding back into old ways of thinking, becoming fearful in general and worried about the future or becoming angry, overwhelmed, or depressed about our situation. If we do slip back into old habits, we can ask for help and turn again to God.

As part of her discussion of asking for help, Mary brings up the profound respect that she and other beings of light have for our free will. To them, it is a kind of higher dimensional "law" they will not override. Although they want to help, they will not intercede on our behalf until we ask. I sense that this is one of the great differences between our third-dimensional world and the higher realms. In our world, people exert power over others all the time without being asked. One of the most common ways is by giving unsolicited advice. There are countless other ways of engaging in domination, mostly based in thinking that we *know* what *should* happen in a particular circumstance, and then we exert our will through our speech and actions, to bring about the desired result. As Gandhi put it, "Any attempt to impose your will on another is an act of violence." Mary concurs with this perspective. She advises us not to exert power over others, but rather to respect their free will, just as is done in the higher realms.

What does this look like in practical terms? Imagine you've just met your friend's new boyfriend, and you have a strong reaction to him. Your impulse might be to tell your friend that she's making a big mistake and to help her see that this man isn't right for her. However, if you wanted to respect your friend's free will, you might instead express that you have concerns about her new relationship and ask if she'd like to hear what they are. You've converted your urge to tell your friend what to do into a request to reveal yourself and discuss your worries with your friend.

In promoting respect for free will, Mary isn't advocating living as though we're entirely independent. This is an important discernment. Many people interpret the admonition to respect others' free will to mean never asking for or giving help. In the previous example, that might look like keeping your opinions to yourself and assuming your friend's choices are none of your business. Such holding back could result in depriving your friend of valuable insight or support. Not revealing your feelings also distances you. The key to respecting free will is to ask if others would like your intervention.

When we want help for ourselves, Mary again urges us to ask; especially, she urges us to ask God for help. However, she also wants us to understand that we can make requests of others without crossing over into coercion—as long as we respect their choice to say yes or no. We adhere to the principle of free will through accepting their right to decide whether or not they want to fulfill our request.

Herein lies another reason for turning to God before we act. If we're already connected to God and experience God's peace, then we have the freedom and strength to accept another person's free choice, including that person's right to say no. Our freedom comes through our connection to God, because in that connection we're already complete and sustained in our essence. We don't depend on other people to fulfill us. We can ask for their help, knowing that if they don't decide to give it, we're still whole and sustained, and we have other options. This awareness brings true freedom, freedom to engage others and freedom to allow them to choose how they will respond.

Another mistake people frequently make is to think that respecting free will means we should be passive and refrain from responding to others. Sometimes we call this being a doormat. The problem is that this attitude doesn't support our own volition. What being respectful of others' free will actually means is not assuming a position of superiority by thinking we know what's best for others, what's right or wrong in a certain situation, or what others *should* be doing. Assumptions like these are all forms of judgment; they are based on ideas of right and wrong. Instead of imposing our judgments on others, we can access our feelings in the situation and then communicate our experience in terms of those feelings. In other words, we can share our concern, anxiety, doubt, alarm, terror, hurt, sadness, despair, or whatever it is. We can express why we're having those feelings—what we think is happening or might happen—and we can *ask* for what we'd like.

Returning to the example of the friend and her new boyfriend, rather than judging him as insensitive and hurtful or her as weak and vulnerable, you could connect with your feelings. Perhaps you feel worried about the way he spoke to her because you want her to be treated with respect and kindness. If so, you might ask your friend if she would be willing to hear your viewpoint and talk with you about your concerns. And if you respect your friend's free will, you will be open to accepting a no.

Accepting others' right to their choices, especially when we don't like those choices, requires great faith. Ultimately, it requires being connected to God enough to know that your essential well-being doesn't reside with others or their actions, even if you are affected by those actions. Acceptance also means releasing the other person to God instead of assuming that we're somehow authorized or entitled to decide for them what they should do. When we assume a position of power over another, we're assuming that they're not sufficiently connected to God and therefore need us to take charge.

It's worth repeating that respecting another's free will requires a deep level of trust in God. I see Mary as embodying such trust. She is helping us to find our own connection to that same trust and live our lives from that basis. She directs us to our higher self, asking that we choose to connect to God before taking action. If the other person says no, we can stay in connection to God and consider other options. We can release our thoughts about how things should happen and let God guide us. We can trust in a higher plan and ask for clarity about how to proceed.

Many people ask how they can respect another's free will if that person is choosing to hurt them or someone else. The question reminds me of a story I heard from a Buddhist teacher. Someone asked him, "What if someone attacks me?" His response was, "Bless that person with all the blessings of the Buddha and then grab your umbrella and defend yourself!"

Marshall Rosenberg describes this kind of response as the protective use of force. In other words, you don't act from a disposition of superiority that is based on ideas of right and wrong and the assumption that you know best; instead, you act from a stance of support for life, basing your actions on love and connection to the Divine. Thus, there may be times when you consciously choose to override another's free will if that seems to be the path most supportive of life. However, in my experience, when I connect to God before acting, I notice that God is amazingly creative in finding ways to take care of me and others, ways that don't involve overriding others' free will or my own.

Mary acknowledges that there are certain circumstances in which we are called upon to act on others' behalf because we're responsible for their well-being to the extent that they're not capable of being responsible for themselves. For example, parents often must intervene in their children's lives. Yet even in these circumstances, she urges us to use our discernment to notice when children have become capable of making their own responsible choices. She calls us to support them in developing their autonomy and capacity for acting responsibly. As soon as they attain that capability, our job is to respect their free will.

I see respect for free will as an essential aspect of parenting or any form of caretaking: we need to be aware of the point at which others are capable of taking care of themselves and no longer need us to act on their behalf. At this point, our role must shift to respect for their choices, as it would with an equal. As parents, we are in service to our children, helping to launch them on their path in God. The difficulty usually occurs when we don't agree with our children's choices—or the choices of anyone we're caring for. That is when we are called upon to shift our perspective, and that shift that can be quite challenging.

I was given a very painful lesson in this arena when my daughter was in her early teens. We had been part of a spiritual community for her entire life, and I was committed to engaging all the recommended spiritual practices and life disciplines, as I believed this was for our highest good. Unfortunately, I was not open to many of my daughter's subtle and not-so-subtle signals that she no longer wanted to participate in this aspect of our lives. Finally, she communicated her desires in a form I could no longer deny or dismiss: she and her best friend ran away from home. Fortunately, they were only gone for just over two days, and then they returned safely. Through the immense anguish of being cut off from contact with my daughter, I was finally forced to see that I was obstructing her well-being by continuing to make choices for her that she no longer wanted or required.

Once our children become competent to make their own choices, it is our role to respect those choices, even if we don't like them. Here again, we need to deal with our own pain—the pain of our loved ones making choices we don't like. And again, we can understand this situation as God reaching out to us, and we can engage in the process of turning to God. When we've fully connected to God and have come to peace, we can take action. We can engage in a dialog with our children, tell them how we feel, and ask them to consider other choices. We can respect their free will to agree with us or not while remaining in our wholeness of connection with God.

Mary closes with a reminder that we are never alone. For me, this is the heart of her communication, the gold at the core. Our habitual response to pain reveals our tendency to assume separation and to act on that basis. Mary calls us to a different assumption—one of connection with God, of trust in God, of opening to and surrender to God. Rather than seeing pain or a no as proof that we've been abandoned, we can see them as God's way of beckoning us and use them as a pathway to reembrace God. Through remembering our unity with God, we can turn to God and ask for help. As Yeshua said, "Ask and it shall be given."

FOUR

The Dark Night of the Soul

Beloved ~

Yes, I want to talk to you about the dark night of the soul. This is a very mysterious concept to many of you. Most of you have a place within you that you're afraid of going, something that brings up too much pain. The dark night of the soul is about facing your fear and pain and going into it rather than avoiding it.

What happens when you do that? It is not what you fear. There is an initial period in which you feel your fear, feel your pain, whatever it is. There is often a feeling of expansion with this, since you usually have shrunk back or contracted away from the pain or fear. There is a sense of relaxing and opening as your feeling nature expands into your whole experience. At some point, often sooner than you would expect, a shift happens. At that point, your experience changes to one of trust and peace, perhaps a sense of being carried— as in carried by a river rather than fighting against the current.

What has happened is that you have connected with the beings of light that are there to support you, to carry you. The pain may or may not go away, but your experience of it is different because you are in the light. The light is stronger—and you are more attracted to it—than your pain. You have entered the River of Light, and it is now cleansing and guiding you.

Your job as humans is to stay in this River of Light. That is your true heart's refuge and calling. It doesn't take you away from life. It takes you into true life. This is the river that truly quenches our thirst.

All people eventually, sooner or later, come to the dark night of the soul. There may be more than one dark night, depending on the person's design for their lifetime, the depth to which they let themselves go into their pain or fear, and the depth with which they connect with the River of Light. All connections with the River of Light are divine gifts that move us further in our path of growing in love and light.

With all my blessings,
I AM Mary Magdalene

*M*ary's discussion of the dark night of the soul continues her instructions from the previous transmission about turning to God when we're in pain and asking for God's help. Now, she gives us an actual step-by-step practice for how to connect with God through fully experiencing our fear and pain.

Mary acknowledges that the dark night of the soul is a mysterious concept for many people. She explains that most of us have a place within our being—some part of ourselves—that we don't want to experience because it brings up too much pain. The dark night of the soul is about facing our fear and pain, about going into it rather than avoiding it. Most of us are afraid to open to our pain because we imagine doing so will invite in too much suffering. We may picture ourselves sinking in a quicksand of agony, possibly becoming so overwhelmed that we die of pain. These deep-seated fears activate our instinct for survival. But in reality, when we go into our pain, something very different occurs.

Mary tells us there's an initial period of simply feeling the pain, which includes feeling the fear associated with it. And so we feel both our fear and our pain. As we continue opening to our feelings, we'll experience a sense of expansion, a sense of relaxing and opening. Where before, out of fear, we contracted or shrank away from the pain, now the contraction begins to unwind and release as it is replaced by expansion, relaxation, and openness. We experience our feeling nature as it extends again into our whole being.

At some point in this process, we undergo a shift as we feel lifted out of our distress. Mary points out that this release often occurs sooner than we expect, countering our tendency to assume that we're going to be stuck in misery without end. Even if the conviction that we will never get beyond the pain does arise, we can boost our faith by remembering that this state is temporary and absolutely will change. I have consistently found that the process works exactly as Mary describes. Even so, during the early stage of opening, I still notice my deep-seated belief that I'll get lost in my anguish and be overwhelmed by suffering. This is why I find it invaluable to be aware that *an integral part of the dark night of the soul is my initial assumption that my pain will last forever.* Now, when that thought arises, I see it as a sign that the process is under way, and I continue to open, knowing that a shift will occur.

What is this shift? Mary describes it perfectly as a shift to trust and peace, perhaps a sense of being carried—as by a river—rather than fighting against the current. I find this description affects me viscerally. I can tangibly feel the transition from a somatic state of fear and contraction to one of trust and peace. I notice that my belly relaxes and my breathing drops lower in my body. My state of growing relaxation is deepened by the image of relaxing my fight against the current and allowing myself to be carried by the river. I feel a sense of lightness and ease, along with the experience of trust and peace.

Mary explains what has occurred: we have connected with beings of light who are literally supporting and carrying us. She calls
this entering the River of Light, an experience that cleanses us of our
fear and guides us. While the pain may or may not go away, we are
changed because we are in the light, and the light is stronger than
the darkness of our pain. As we are drawn to experience the light,
our pain will inevitably recede, if not go away altogether.

I picture the original pain and accompanying fear as a pitch-black
cave. The cave represents the dark night of the soul. When we choose
to open to pain, we choose to enter into the shadows of the cavity.
Stepping inside, we allow our consciousness to expand to the cavern's
full dimensions. We feel its cool, moist surfaces. We may still fear
that the darkness and the unknown will overwhelm us, yet another
part of us whispers that opening to the cave is the best option and
urges us to trust the process. We begin to have a sense of letting go
and relaxation as we release our resistance to experiencing whatever
exists here. At a certain point, we're drawn to the other side of the
cave, which opens into a River of Light. We give ourselves to the
river, experiencing a great depth of trust and peace. As we let ourselves be carried by the beings of light that form this river, we're
cleansed and guided to where we need to be. Our pain becomes
more distant as the light of the river replaces the darkness of our
fear.

The process Mary describes reminds me of Elisabeth Kübler-
Ross's model of the stages of grief that people experience in coming
to terms with death. These stages—denial, anger, bargaining, depression, and acceptance—seem similar to Mary's description of the
first part of the dark night of the soul, where we expand into the
cave of our fears and eventually come to acceptance. Mary's elucida-
tion of opening to the light reminds me of accounts of people at the
edge of death who have seen angels or various manifestations of

light and experienced great bliss and peace. Mary suggests that we can have these experiences not only at death, but during life as well.

In fact, Mary tells us that the River of Light takes us into "true life" and that our job as humans is to stay in the river. She's not just talking about an isolated, one-time event. The River of Light is a state we can continue to experience. In so doing, she tells us, we realize our true heart's refuge and calling, which "truly quenches our thirst."

Just hearing Mary's description stokes my longing for union with this river and for the place in my heart to which it connects me. I feel the trust and peace the river carries us to. It's a place I know in my soul, and yet the path there still surprises me: that surrendering into pain leads to such beauty. I'm heartened by the awareness that each time I engage this process of letting go into pain, I'm strengthened in my ability to stay connected to the River of Light. Residing in this river has become my spiritual path.

I believe that opening fully into any moment will take us to the River of Light and the heart's refuge. And yet, pain is a particular gift for supporting us to merge with our experience. It's like an alarm that keeps going off to remind us that something's not right. If we heed the warning, pain provides a unique form of help, guiding us all the way through to our very depths and beyond. However, our painful places are also the ones that most of us tend to avoid. Mary points to our avoidance of pain as the biggest stumbling block to uniting with God. I think that's why she's so insistent about focusing on pain in her communications. She sees we need it. Merging fully with our experience, to the point of total unity or oneness, is the way through to our next step in spiritual evolution. And because it's a process of surrender, it's a particularly Feminine path she's bringing forth—for both men and women.

Mary makes it clear that, sooner or later, everyone will experience at least one dark night of the soul. She urges us to recognize it as a doorway and make good use of it. As her final words affirm, "All connections with the River of Light are divine gifts that move us further in our path of growing in love and light."

Figure 4-1. OPENING TO PAIN

1. Notice you're in pain.

2. Choose to fully experience and open to the pain.

3. Merge with the pain by relaxing and expanding into it.

4. Allow the pain to take you to Source (inner divine qualities).

5. Experience the shift into peace as you begin to flow with the River of Light.

6. Rest in connection to God.

7. Let God direct your actions.

PART II

Intimacy and Spirituality

FIVE

The Divine Gift of Sexuality

Good day, beloveds ~

Today I wish to speak with you about sexuality. This is such an important area of your humanness. Sexuality is a great gift from God. Many have tried to convince you that it is sinful or wrong or evil, but nothing could be farther from the truth. Sexuality is a divine gift. It is an opportunity for you to experience the merging of your physical self, your energetic self, your heart, and your consciousness with another person and with the Divine. It is a great beauty, a sacrament of love. Do you think the Creator would begin the life of a new being with an act that was sinful or evil? No, it is a celebration of life and union with God. It is a great and beautiful act of devotion and love.

For this to be so, however, it must be engaged in love, with a partner whom you love and with whom you can fully open your heart. This requires love and safety. If the love and safety aren't there, you can still engage in the physical act of being sexual, and to some extent the energetic aspects, but you will not experience it as divine union. It will simply be a release, a letting go of tension, a brief numbing out of your sense of craving. What you are craving is the full union of yourself, on all levels, with the Divine. You know that union in your deepest memory, as that is where we all come from originally. That desire for reunion is always motivating you. It moves you to join with a partner sexually and also to join in life as partners, spouses, or whatever you may term it.

It is good that you remember that union and seek to re-create it. Understand, though, that first you must create it within yourself. This world, in and of itself, will never satisfy you. You must first find your joy and ecstasy through your own union with the Divine. This requires prayer, or communicating with God, and meditation, or resting in God's embrace, fully surrendering to God. It may also require healing and dissolving any blocks you have to divine union—physically, emotionally, mentally, or spiritually. There is no limit or barrier to our joy, ecstasy, and peace in God. It does not require a partner. It is always available to us, at all times and places and in all circumstances.

So this must be the platform from which you enter into sexual union. You must come already full. And you must enter into the container of love and safety with your partner. If the love and safety are not there, then you do not have a container for true union, and you will be hurting yourself and the other.

In this world, you are always moving toward God or away from God. Nothing is static or neutral. If your desire is to always be moving into divine union, you must choose and engage that, and it includes your sexuality. Then it is a gift and blessing that will grow you, your partner, and the world in love and beauty and joy and light. There are many ways to bring forth your blessings of love and light. Sexuality is one such way, a very beautiful and sacred way.

I send you my fullest blessings and deep heart-love.
I AM Mary Magdalene

Although most spiritual teachers don't address the topic of sexuality, it's an area that interests many people, and in this transmission Mary ventured further into it. I find her passion for sexuality to be inspiring and courageous; she easily could be written off as "nonspiritual" for so much as speaking about sexuality, let alone declaring it an intrinsic part of the spiritual path. Indeed, that may be a part of what happened in the past. My sense is that Mary has been biding her time until the present moment, when the energies of human consciousness have shifted to include the Feminine as partner to the Masculine. The Feminine manifests as vibratory energy—as the energy of creation, sustenance, and dissolution. It is the endless cycle of life arising, growing, changing, releasing, and arising again. And one of the most powerful forms of energy we humans know is the energy of sexuality. Mary acknowledges that sexual energy has been seen as negative. When she says, "Many have tried to convince you that [sexuality] is sinful or wrong or evil," she is gently alluding to the many religious institutions and teachings that for centuries have espoused the sinfulness of sexuality, calling it the work of the devil and promoting abstinence as a spiritual path.

This devaluation of sexuality is a result of the Masculine's estrangement from the Feminine. The Masculine is not about sexuality at all: rather, it is about the purity that transcends all arising and all manifestation and its accompanying transcendental consciousness. Various traditions refer to this state and consciousness as the void, emptiness, pure consciousness, the "Self," or the unmanifest. One way of connecting with the Masculine is to think of it as the quality most people seek in meditation: the stillness, spaciousness, and silence we experience when the mind becomes quiet. I also like to picture the Masculine as the void of the universe prior to the big bang (the Feminine!).

For a long time, most spiritual paths and teachings have been primarily Masculine-oriented traditions that have tended to condemn sexuality as an obstacle to spirituality. This degradation of sexuality has affected not only our relationship to sexuality, but—because women are often equated with sexuality—it affects attitudes toward women as well. And the very act of opposing the natural drive of our sexual energy has only added fuel to this association. The result: within Masculine-oriented spirituality (and Masculine cultures, in general), sexuality and women tend to be linked, and both are devalued and repressed.

At the esoteric level, there's an explanation for this. For a long time, Earth has been primarily under the influence of a specific ray of God-Light, which I call the First Ray of divine will and power. Its function is to bring aspects of the Divine Masculine onto Earth. This ray strengthens and supports the use of our will and intention to live a spiritual life and to carry out God's plan for us. It has influenced our primarily Masculine orientation for the last several thousand years.

Now, along with the First Ray, the Second and Third Rays of God-Light are beginning to shine upon Earth. The Second Ray is the Divine Feminine ray of love, and the Third Ray is the Divine Child ray of wisdom in action. We are entering into a new period of the unity of these three rays. One of the ways this unity will manifest is through integration of the Feminine—including women and sexual energy—into our spirituality and spiritual beliefs. We've already seen enormous changes over the last fifty years, in which many religious structures have become more inclusive of women and couples. The next frontier is the embrace of sexuality itself as sacred.

Mary affirms the sacred nature of sexuality at the beginning of this communication. She calls sexuality a divine gift from God, a great beauty, a sacrament of love, a celebration of life and union

Figure 5-1. CHARACTERISTICS OF
THE DIVINE MASCULINE AND FEMININE

Divine Masculine	*Divine Feminine*

TRANSCENDENCE	**RADIANCE**
That which is prior to space, time, and all arising	*Vibratory energy of manifestation*

QUALITIES

Peace · Transcendence · Emptiness	Creativity · Wisdom · Fullness · Bliss
Stillness · Presence	Motion · Energy · Change
Liberation · Freedom	Birth · Life · Death
Already ascended	Already descended
Awareness · Insight	Love · Harmony
Transcending time/space	Arising, evolving, and disintegrating in time/space

ACTIONS

Descending	Ascending
Yang · Hot	Yin · Cool
Assertive · Penetrating	Receptive · Surrendering
Active · Doing	Passive · Being
Challenge · Willpower	Nurture · Support
Focused, mental attention	Divergent, feeling-based attention
Goal-oriented	Relationship- and quality-of-life-oriented

IN HUMANS

Mind, will, and intention	Body, energy, sexuality, and emotions

Most Exalted Form:	*Most Exalted Form:*
CONSCIOUSNESS	**LOVE**

with God, and a great and beautiful act of devotion and love. Her words conjure up images from the world of art—the *Venus de Milo*, Michelangelo's *David*, the *Mona Lisa*, and countless paintings and sculptures of sensual and erotic art from around the world—along with the primal energy of love.

Mary clarifies for us that sexuality provides an opportunity to experience the merging of our physical and energetic selves, our hearts, and our consciousness with another person and with the Divine. In one sentence, she clarifies the entire purpose of sacred sexuality. I celebrate her mastery in concisely and perfectly expressing the mission statement for such an elusive topic. The key principle of her statement is *merging*. Merging, an essentially Feminine expression, contrasts with Masculine ways of engaging the will and intention to achieve a goal. The Feminine is expressed through opening, surrendering, allowing, and merging.

Again, I marvel at Mary's brilliance and simplicity when she asks us, "Do you think the Creator would begin the life of a new being with an act that was sinful or evil?" If there is any doubt left that sexuality is somehow dirty or sinful, I see her removing it with this question. For me, this simple question speaks volumes, and the answer is inherently clear.

Mary shifts focus, then, telling us that sacred sexuality requires a container of love and safety so that we can fully open our hearts. Otherwise, she says, our sexuality is only a tension-release and a brief numbing out of our sense of craving.

Whew, she doesn't mess around! That's part of what I love about her. According to Mary, our sexual craving is really a desire for total reuniting with God and All That Is. We already remember this state of connectedness because it is where we came from and what we're longing to return to. In our sexuality, we allow ourselves to experience this yearning for reconnection. And, in fact, sexuality

can be a means of re-creating divine union. For this to be so, however, it must occur within a container of love and safety.

I find it interesting that Mary specifies that love and safety are
the necessary container. Most of us have a sense of what it's like
when sexuality is linked to love, at least the third-dimensional manifestation of love. However, I'm surprised to hear her say that safety
is a prerequisite for sacred sexuality. She uses the word *safety* rather
than *commitment* or *marriage*, which are the common ways people
try to create safety. *Safety* implies something larger, something that
can be created in a variety of ways. At the same time, I hear the
focus she puts on love and safety as a voice upholding the Feminine

Figure 5-2. THE FIRST THREE RAYS OF GOD-LIGHT

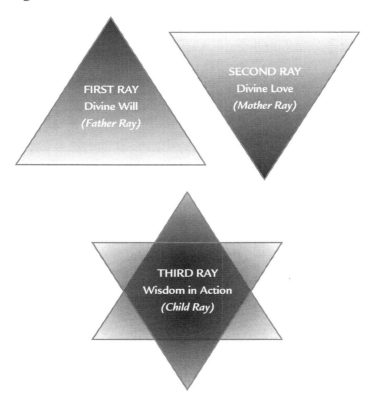

requirements for opening and merging. This emphasis contrasts with the Masculine approach, in which neither love nor safety is considered an essential part of sexuality.

We all contain both the Masculine and the Feminine within ourselves, so I want to emphasize that I'm not referring to men when I say *masculine* or to women when I say *feminine*. When I, as a woman, have engaged in sexuality without the full container of love and safety, I have been led by my masculine side. And the results of those choices left my feminine side unfulfilled.

This leads to Mary's next point, that the primary prerequisite or foundation for sacred sexuality is the creation of a union of the inner Masculine and Feminine. For many of us, the process of self-reintegration involves opening up to, and getting to know, parts of our Masculine or our Feminine that we have suppressed or disassociated from. We may need to strengthen these parts of ourselves so that they are in balance and full within our own selves.

I was in my midforties when I began to fully embrace the path of sacred sexuality. I realized at that time that I had previously adapted to a goal-oriented, Masculine form of sexuality, which could even be described as athletic. I was primarily focused on pleasing my partner, and I measured my "success" by how passionately I responded to him: how many orgasms I had, how long they lasted, and how strong or intense my experience was. I realized that if I were to take my partner and all my performing out of the picture, I really didn't know my own sexuality. This intrigued me, and I spent the next year getting to know myself sexually: what my sexual drives and delights were, what it was to follow my own sexual energy, and where it led me. In the process, my feminine sexuality blossomed, and I came to treasure that part of myself.

Mary emphasizes the importance of our inner union with the Divine. We'll never be satisfied, she tells us, if we seek union in the world—including through relationships—without the foundation of our inner union. Truly, the union we seek through sexuality is always available to us, with or without a partner and with or without engaging our sexuality. Sexuality is simply one method of union. And for sexuality to be fulfilling, we first need to be complete within ourselves—already in union with God and abiding within a container of love and safety.

Perhaps you're thinking what a tall order this is. I agree, especially given the way most of us were raised and the cultural patterns that reinforce our alienation from ourselves—and especially our Feminine aspect—as well as from God. But what else are we here to do if not to grow and heal and open to union with God? And the path of sexuality is such a gift, such an alluring path to knowing God.

There is tremendous wisdom in Mary's closing statement that we in this world are always moving toward God or away from God and that nothing is static or neutral. I hear it as a call to action. We must enlist the Masculine within us to keep us moving toward God. If we choose to engage God through our sexuality, Mary assures us it will be "a gift and blessing that will grow you, your partner, and the world in love and beauty and joy and light." I feel blessed and inspired by that message, and deeply grateful.

SIX

My Sacred Relationship with Yeshua

Dear one of my heart ~

Today, I would like to tell you about me. I am Mary Magdalene. There is much confusion about me amongst many people, debate about who I was, what I was, what my relationship to Yeshua was. Much of the debate is a reflection of those who are debating. They see me through the filter of their beliefs and perceptions. They see me the way they see themselves and project onto me what they believe about themselves.

In truth, I was Yeshua's sacred partner. We were equals, as holy man and woman, holy husband and wife. Just as there is no separation within our Mother-Father God—both aspects are equal and yet truly beyond equality, simply two faces of the Divine Being—so were Yeshua and I. We loved each other completely and still do. We saw each other as the divine self. We both were prepared for our meeting and relationship with each other, through the many schools and traditions of our times. My training was primarily through the Egyptian temple of Isis, where I was trained as a high priestess. There were many forms of being a priestess in this lineage. Many involved healing and blessing work. I was trained in the highest arts of serving the Divine through what was called Sacred Relationship. This was a school, or stream, within the temple, a very high one.

I was trained to relate to all of life as the play of God, the manifestation of God. And I was raised and trained to see all the parts of myself as holy and sacred—my physical body, emotional body, mental body, etheric body, and my higher self, or spiritual bodies. Upon this foundation, I was also trained to relate to a partner as the Divine Being and through that relationship to engage with that partner in practices and an entire sacred life that allowed each of us, each partner, to fulfill his or her divine blueprint of serving light and love in this world.

As a practitioner of Sacred Relationship, my design or chosen form (chosen by my soul before my incarnation at the time you know me from) was to engage Sacred Relationship with Yeshua and, through him, with all beings. He likewise chose—through his soul's design and in concert with all the beings of light and our Mother-Father God—to engage Sacred Relationship with me and all beings. It was appropriate for that time and place that I should engage Sacred Relationship directly with Yeshua and indirectly with the world, and that he should engage Sacred Relationship directly with both me and the world.

Now the time has changed as we are entering into a new age, the age of Aquarius. It has been said by many that this is the age of equality between the Masculine and the Feminine, and this is true. And for this shift into equality to occur, there is a particular kind of passage required at this time. It is as though you are giving birth to the new age. As has always been the case with birth, this is uniquely the domain of the Feminine. It is the Feminine that must come to the fore and take the lead for this birth into the new age of equality to occur. And so I have been called to become very active at this time, to come forth to many to support this birth process, to support the Sacred Feminine coming forth, assuming her true power and place beside the Sacred Masculine. This is a call to all women and men, for all have the Sacred Feminine within them, as all have the Sacred Masculine, too. And it is a call to women and men in different ways.

For women, it is a call to assume your power, the Feminine power. The Feminine is the power of love and strength. We all know the strength it takes to birth a child. And it takes great strength to raise a child, as well. The Feminine is the complement to the Masculine. Both have their strengths, and both are required for wholeness. The Feminine brings life energy, love, aliveness, wisdom, faith, receptivity to the Divine, feeling, and inclusiveness. The Masculine brings insight, understanding, awareness, direction, tracking or maintaining awareness, attaining goals, and carrying out the divine plan. Each person contains all these qualities within them, as we all contain the Masculine and the Feminine within. And most people also resonate more fully with one or the other of these qualities, the Masculine or the Feminine. And so one option is to manifest this in life through Sacred Relationship with a partner.

Sacred Relationship is natural to humans, because of the way that we came to be here. We all came from the undifferentiated Source, or Oneness, which many call God. I use the term Supreme Creator. From the Supreme Creator came the first manifestation, a kind of step-down from Supreme Creator at the first level, which was Mother-Father God. All other beings and forms on Earth came through this first division into form. You could say that in some ways all beings on Earth are "children" of Mother-Father God. This isn't literal because it is at a level of high physics that most people do not understand. I am giving you this as an analogy, simply to say that the pattern of Sacred Relationship is imprinted into your souls from this original manifestation that you are all the "offspring" of.

This does not mean that everyone needs to find a partner. Everyone can find Sacred Relationship within themselves. Indeed, each individual must find this whether they are with a partner or not. This wholeness within oneself is essential as the foundation for Sacred Relationship with a partner. One of the reasons there is so much difficulty and struggle in relationships today is that many have not found that wholeness within themselves and are looking to their partner—or a desired partner if they're not yet in relationship—to make them whole. This is backward and will never work. People are not ready to enter into Sacred Relationship with a partner until they have found wholeness within themselves through the union and balancing of their own Masculine and Feminine and their union with God. On this basis, one comes to relationship whole, already full. Then one has love and light to offer a partner. Then there is excess to create the new union of their sacred partnership.

A sacred partnership is a kind of alchemy. You are mixing your destinies of service to God, of bringing love and light into the world. A true sacred partnership increases the love and light that the couple is bringing into the world, such that it is greater than the two could bring as individuals. That is sacred alchemy: it increases the love and light that both have to bring to the world through their relationship.

And so, to return to my relationship with Yeshua, we were in Sacred Relationship with each other, and this included sacred sexual relationship. We were both prepared for this through the training we received individually through sacred traditions, especially the Egyptian and Indian sacred paths. We engaged in lovemaking as a process of transforming our bodies into light and love, in service to our destinies. And we were deeply in love with each other. We lived this love through all aspects of our lives, and both of us were dedicated to the work that Yeshua was the leader for.

Today, as two thousand years ago, we are dedicated to supporting all humans in this process of upliftment and growth in God's love and light. The form has evolved, but the calling and core is the same. I am devoted to being a kind of midwife at this time of the next phase of this Grand Plan, and thus I come to you with my messages in support of that.

I love you most fully and openheartedly.
I AM Mary Magdalene

This was the first time that Mary spoke in detail about herself and her relationship with Yeshua (Jesus). In the previous messages, I sensed she had refrained from speaking about herself or Yeshua because she wanted us to focus on our transformation at this current time—and what we need to do to support that—rather than on information about Mary and Yeshua's lives.

I believe she chose to talk about her intimate relationship with Yeshua now to inspire us and show us what's possible in the arena of Sacred Relationship. In the past, esoteric practices of Sacred Relationship—especially those linked to sexuality—were frequently reserved for select initiates and were usually kept secret. Mary's revelation of this aspect of her relationship with Yeshua feels like a sacred offering. It's as though we're being taken into the inner chamber of a temple that's generally open only to practitioners. I believe she granted us this access because each person who understands and accepts the true nature of her relationship with Yeshua contributes to the power and effectiveness of their union, even now. I also think that Mary is laying the foundation for us to consider this particular form of sacred engagement as part of our spiritual path.

Mary begins by plainly stating who she is: "I am Mary Magdalene." She then refers to all the debate about who she is and her relationship to Yeshua, saying that a lot of confusion exists because people project their own beliefs about themselves and their world onto her. I'm struck by Mary's graciousness in this simple statement. She spends no time or energy on defending herself or criticizing others for what has been said about her—let alone done to her. Rather, she focuses on enabling us to understand why she's been portrayed as a sinner, prostitute, and so on, so that we can let go of any negative characterizations that might block us from receiving her help. Her explanation also points to the dangers of projecting our beliefs and perceptions onto others.

Mary beautifully describes her relationship with Yeshua as "holy man and woman, holy husband and wife." She tells us that they loved each other completely, as equals, and saw each other as the divine self. This was supported by her training in the Egyptian temple of Isis as a high priestess in the practice of Sacred Relationship. There she learned to relate to every aspect of life as a manifestation of God— and to see all the parts of herself as sacred: her physical, emotional, mental, and etheric bodies, and her higher self or spiritual bodies.

Mary's list of all her different bodies corresponds to my understanding of what might be called esoteric anatomy. Our physical body, which is just one of the forms of our manifestation, has the densest frequency and is supported by our etheric (or energy) body. At progressively subtler frequencies, we also have an emotional body and a mental body. These four together comprise our four lower bodies, the bodies we most easily connect with in third-dimensional reality. Most people in the third-dimensional world are, at least to some extent, aware of their physical bodies, emotions, thoughts, and energy.

Beyond these four lower bodies, we have our higher self, which is made up of the causal body and spiritual body. The causal body, also called the soul, is the part of the self that continues from lifetime to lifetime. It gives us our sense of I, or identification with the self. Often described as the body of cause and effect, it is the repository from which we create our reality through our thoughts, feelings, and actions. This body contains the knowledge of all past and present incarnations and is the source of our still small voice, or conscience, which guides us to follow our values and life purpose.

Our spiritual body is the source of our connection to the Divine. This body includes our I AM presence, or our individual connection to and manifestation of Source, as well as our indwelling divine consciousness.

Figure 6-1. THE SIX BODIES OF OUR ESOTERIC ANATOMY

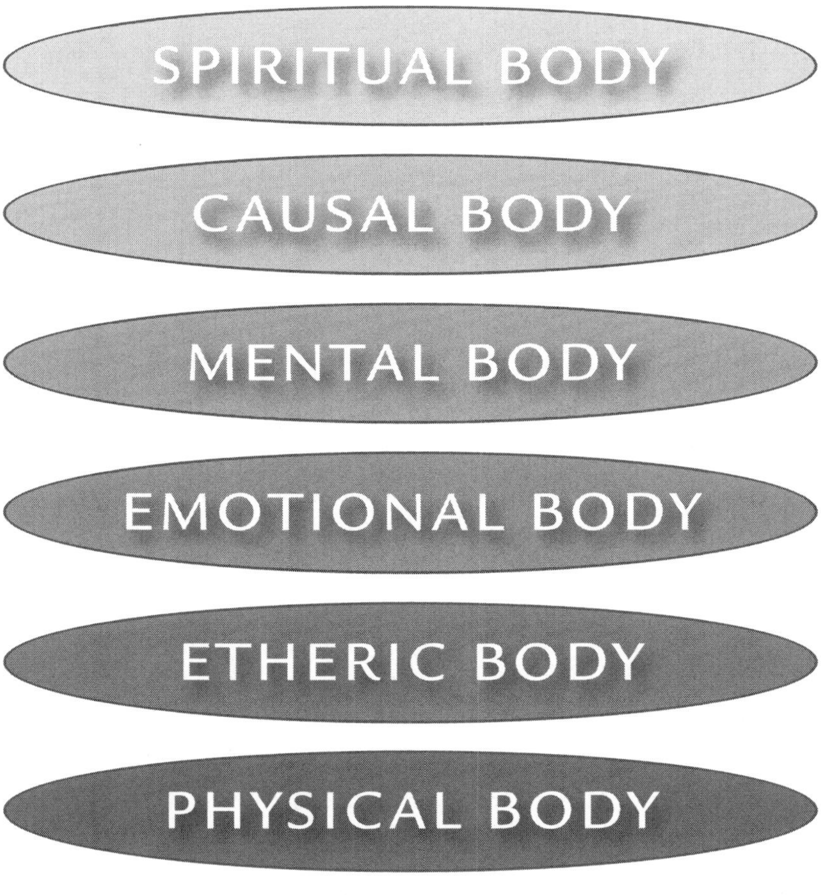

SPIRITUAL BODY

CAUSAL BODY

MENTAL BODY

EMOTIONAL BODY

ETHERIC BODY

PHYSICAL BODY

At this point in our spiritual evolution, many teachers point to the necessity of purifying our four lower bodies so that we can move into the dimensions of higher consciousness beyond the third dimension. Because so many of us were trained to suppress our emotions, the emotional body is the body most in need of help. A big part of Mary's gift to us is her explicit and detailed instruction on how to work with emotions so that we may be fully empowered to move into our next phase of spiritual development.

After being trained to see herself as divine, Mary was instructed in how to relate to a partner as a manifestation of the Divine Being. All this training formed the foundation for her and Yeshua's engagement of Sacred Relationship. She tells us that these practices allowed each of them to fulfill their divine blueprint of serving light and love in this world.

I understand the term *divine blueprint* in two ways. In one meaning, Mary and Yeshua were fulfilling the blueprint they chose before they were born, the blueprint for what they would bring into their lives and how they would manifest their divine purpose. The other meaning of *divine blueprint* is that she and Yeshua acted as a blueprint for all beings, showing us how to serve the manifestation of light and love in this world.

Mary demonstrates how purposefully she has engaged her role of serving humanity. In her lifetime, two thousand years ago, her mission was specifically tailored to a time when women were considered socially and politically inferior to men. Because of the barriers women experienced, her chosen path was to relate to Yeshua as the Divine and, through him, to relate to the whole world as divine. Yeshua, as a man, was allowed a direct relationship with all beings, as well as with Mary. Their paths were different.

Mary clarifies that, as we enter the age of Aquarius—which is characterized by equality between the Masculine and Feminine—

the status of women has changed. Now, women are called to come forward and take their place beside men as equals, with the same relationship to the world as men.

As Mary points out, giving birth has always been the domain of women. Now, as all of us are involved in the birth of this new age of the Feminine coming forth to join the Masculine, she is called to help midwife this shift. I believe this is why she is appearing to so many people at this time. It explains why she has "suddenly" moved to the forefront of the spiritual world, why she's so expressive and impassioned about people receiving her communications, and why she is moved to help us with the specific forms of spiritual guidance we require at this juncture in our evolution. Not only are we giving birth to the emergence of the long-suppressed Feminine, but the Feminine is being called forth to guide and support this birth process. And Mary emphasizes, yet again, that this change is as much for men as it is for women. That is because creating equality and unity with our own Feminine and Masculine is first and foremost an inner change.

I greatly appreciate Mary's descriptions of the complementary qualities and strengths of our inner Masculine and Feminine. The Feminine brings life energy, love, aliveness, wisdom, faith, receptivity to the Divine, feeling, and inclusiveness. By contrast, the Masculine brings insight, understanding, awareness along with tracking or maintaining it, direction, attaining goals, and carrying out the divine plan. Clearly, we need both aspects to be whole, but most of us resonate more with the Masculine or the Feminine aspect, and this is specifically why Sacred Relationship can be such a valuable path.

I picture the process of human evolution that Mary describes as a kind of original cell division that created the first appearance of form. All of manifestation came through the initial division of the

Undifferentiated Oneness into Mother-Father God, which is why the pattern of Masculine and Feminine is imprinted on our souls.

Because the Feminine aspect in Christianity was suppressed for so long, the deity became exclusively a Father God, and today Christians generally don't accept the concept of a Mother-Father God. I personally don't think this domination by the Masculine was Yeshua's orientation or teaching, but rather something that occurred after his lifetime, when the Feminine was written out of the official presentation of Christianity. I also notice that Mary uses the terms Father-Mother God and Mother-Father God interchangeably, which reinforces the equality and fluidity between those roles or parts of the Divine.

Relating to a Mother-Father God has been tremendously healing for me. Having been raised as a Jew within a Christian society, I knew God as an exclusively male God and visualized him as the classic old, bearded man in heaven. In my late teens, I became attracted to Eastern spirituality, and I now believe a part of that appeal was the neutral depiction of the Divine. In these traditions, the Divine wasn't a gendered being but was related to as the Absolute, Oneness, Ultimate Reality, and Supreme Being.

Later, I became sensitized to the many ways that religions have suppressed and even demonized both women and the Feminine principle, including portraying the human body, sexuality, and emotions as sinful or nonspiritual. For me, as for many women at this time, the degradation of the Feminine isn't just an aspect of remote history. I have remembered past lifetimes in which I was tortured and killed for my Feminine spirituality, and I am acutely aware of all the ways the Feminine is not valued and celebrated in our world. Because of my early interpretation of "God" as an exclusively Masculine deity and my deep discomfort at the suppression of the Feminine, for most of my life I couldn't bring myself to use the term *God* for the Divine.

Figure 6-2. GOD AND GODDESS IN YAB-YUM

When I encountered the term *Mother-Father God*, I experienced a great "ah-ha" moment and an opening. That simple phrase suddenly made it possible for me to relate to God both as beyond gender and also inclusive of gender in the form of unity and equality. Seeing God in this larger way freed me from my previous reaction and my limited perception of God. A mental picture I have for this new understanding of God is the classic Tantric image of a masculine deity in sexual embrace with a feminine deity, seated in the meditative pose known as *yab-yum*. Not only does this image capture the love and parity between these two aspects of God, it does so in the classically Feminine form of depicting sexual embrace as a metaphor for union with All That Is.

Mary clarifies that we have a choice about whether to engage Sacred Relationship with a partner through sexual union or as a solo practice of integrating our inner Feminine and Masculine. Regardless of which way we do it, we all need to unite our inner Feminine and Masculine. As she points out, this inner union is the foundation of a successful relationship with another. Without it, relationships will be difficult because we will try to get from the other what we truly need to find within ourselves. When we approach relationships from the foundation of our own inner unity, we bring an abundance of love and light instead of a sense of deficiency we hope our partner will fill.

Mary gives us a wonderful depiction of Sacred Relationship as alchemy, describing this alchemy as "mixing your destinies of service to God, of bringing love and light into the world." It evokes for me an image of two chalices of wine being poured together, mingling the liquids to create love and light. The idea of sharing destinies of service to God and bringing love and light into the world powerfully draws me into the depths of what she's describing. This alchemy goes beyond simply sharing physical intimacy or sexual energy. For me, the profundity of her words lifts this practice out of the realm of the merely physical or sexual and into the sublime.

Mary portrays her lovemaking with Yeshua as a process of transforming their bodies into light and love, in service to their destinies. Here, I see the light and love produced from the blending of the wine taking on human form. Beings of love arise within the light, and those beings are themselves composed of light.

Mary provides important insights into the essence of sacred sexuality. In the Egyptian tradition, sacred sexuality was a step-by-step practice for transforming one's energy body into the light of God and connecting fully with one's spiritual body. Again, this could be either a solo practice or it could also involve partnership. Both paths use the transformative power of sexual energy, directed in specific ways, to reach a higher level of being.

Finally, Mary emphasizes that she and Yeshua were deeply in love with each other. They lived this love through every aspect of their lives and brought it to the world through Yeshua's work. Their relationship was a form of divine communion and transformation, in which they related to everything as God and engaged in sexual practices for fully manifesting their divine form and destiny. Both were—and still are—entirely dedicated to transforming and uplifting humans into God's light and love. They chose to engage sacred relationship and sacred sexuality as one pathway for creating this transformation. And so may we, if we so choose.

Ultimately, what really matters is not whether Mary and Yeshua were married or had a sexual relationship or whether we ourselves choose to engage in sacred sexuality. What is essential is being uplifted and growing in God's love and light, as they themselves lived and offer to others. That growth is what Mary values above all and what she supports in all of us in whatever way it manifests. And for that, I am extremely grateful.

PART III

The Nature of Reality

SEVEN

Beyond Doubt

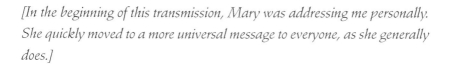

[In the beginning of this transmission, Mary was addressing me personally. She quickly moved to a more universal message to everyone, as she generally does.]

Dear one ~

You are filled with doubt. You doubt that I could be speaking to you. You doubt that higher beings, ascended masters, or angels exist. You doubt anything that's not physically manifest in your third-dimensional world.

It is natural that you should feel and think this way, as this is the way you have been raised. This is the way most of the world thinks at this time. It is a result of the dominance of science, which is really a kind of mass religion in this time. You have been trained to think that only those things that you perceive with your five senses are real, and everything else is unreal. Oddly, you don't perceive your thoughts with your five senses, yet you also trust those. Most of you are ruled by your thoughts, but your thoughts do not serve you very well much of the time.

It is a vast challenge to break out of the confines of this kind of thinking. It is as though a huge barrier has been placed between you and the greater world, leading you to doubt information and experiences you receive that would open you to what is greater. There are reasons why this has been taught and upheld as a way of thinking, which have to do with control of the masses. But what is important is that you have a choice. You are choosing to accept the mass belief system that only your sensory data in the physical world is real. You are choosing to limit your experiences, your awareness, and your consciousness by restricting your field of input to this arena. You could make a different choice. And that choice would change your life.

I tell you that there are higher beings, and that we are real. We want to help you. There are many beings here to help and support you. And you yourself are also a higher being. All of you have a higher self. This is the reality that your leaders and those in control don't want you to know because you are powerful as your higher self. Once you are connected to your higher self, you will not be easy to control. It is somewhat like your movie *The Matrix*. You have a choice to take the red pill or the blue pill. You are already taking one, and that pill is telling you that all the talk and ideas you hear that are beyond the physical are "woo-woo," not trustable, silly, just an illusion. But in that movie, the main character is given a choice: He chooses to take the other pill, and suddenly his perception and awareness are changed and he understands things very differently. Suddenly, he has new abilities and powers.

You do not need to take a pill. (Indeed, most of the pills and drugs you take interfere with this process.) The ability is already within you. You simply need to choose it and release the blocks that are in place within you that veil this reality. The work of releasing those blocks is necessary. Those blocks are at the physical, emotional, mental, and etheric levels. Today, I am addressing the mental blocks, the ideas and beliefs that limit you and keep you bound to a physically based reality, that keep you disconnected from your higher self.

There are other things that can help you to release your mental blocks. Meditation is one. In meditation, you learn to quiet your lower mind, which allows you to open to pure awareness and into the depth of consciousness. In this space, you are available to receive God's embrace, as your lower mind is no longer blocking you.

Hearing the ideas of others who have gone beyond their mental blocks can also support you, because then you may realize that your belief system is just one way of relating to the world and that there are other possibilities, other options. This supports you in choosing a different way of relating to the world.

It is especially helpful to be in the company of one who transmits the power and state of higher consciousness. You can feel this because your body opens, your mind relaxes, your heart is filled with love, and you experience the joy of greater connection to God. This sometimes happens through a group, such as a church. However, churches often combine this transmission with dogma, beliefs that don't necessarily support this God consciousness. Part of honing and developing your mind is to strengthen your discernment so that you do not take on beliefs that don't serve you and that are not aligned to reality. Allow yourself to receive the transmission of unity with God, and maintain the ability to discern the difference between that transmission and any beliefs that are being attached to it. Test the beliefs to see if they seem accurate to your experiences—to see if they open your body, relax your mind, fill your heart with love, and connect you with God. If the beliefs support fear, separation, guilt, blame, or other qualities like these, they are not to be trusted.

Beloved ones, you are courageous at these times to go beyond the mass beliefs. It takes great strength to do this, as many are threatened by those who do not believe the way they do. Love these ones, but do not be limited by their desire to have you support them by thinking as they do. It is not necessary. You never support anyone by limiting yourself.

I invite you to join me and the many beings of light who are here to support you, help you, and love you. We invite you into the vast space of love and freedom in God that we enjoy. It is beautiful here. And you do not have to leave where you are to join us. But you will have to open your minds. Your doubt is limiting you. We do not ask you to believe anything. Simply let go of your doubt and notice what you experience. We are right here, and we love you profoundly.

In love and light,
I AM Mary Magdalene

*A*t the time of this communication, I was experiencing my habitual pattern of self-doubt that surfaces whenever I'm feeling spiritually weak. Mary used my experience of doubt as a springboard to discuss the ideas and beliefs that block our spiritual growth and keep us disconnected from our higher self.

First, she accurately pinpoints all the ways my doubt was manifesting, including my doubt that she could be speaking to me, my doubt about the existence of higher beings, and my doubt about anything that's not physically manifest in my third-dimensional world. It's humorous to me now as I write this how, in three short sentences, she so masterfully summarizes my own personal universe of doubt. And I know this transmission isn't just addressing me, because this kind of doubt plagues many of us. Even though I've experienced the reality of spiritual phenomena on countless occasions, I still manage to doubt the existence of nonphysical reality at times. I'm deeply impressed by the tenacity of this mental habit.

Mary's compassion stands out as she goes on to explain how natural it is that we should think this way: it's how we've been trained. This conditioning comes from what she refers to as the "mass religion" of science, which tells us that only our sensory information is real. She then astutely points out the incongruity of how we relate to our thoughts. Even though our thoughts are often distinct and separate from any physical data we receive from our senses, we don't tend to doubt them or consider them unreal. In fact, most of us are consumed with our thoughts and relate to them as the most real part of our world.

For example, if someone says something that disturbs us, the actual incident may last for only a matter of seconds, but we may spend hours or days thinking about the remark. We may replay the scene in our minds, have an imaginary conversation with the person in which we defend ourselves or retaliate. We may analyze why the incident occurred, plan what to do about it, or perhaps just ruminate about related incidents from the past and project various scenarios into the future. This doesn't happen only when we're upset; that's just when we tend to be aware of it. Actually, it's going on most of the time. If you don't believe it, try meditating and notice what your mind does. Most people's minds are very busy with a constant progression of thoughts. It's easy to notice this when you're sitting still and trying to quiet and focus your mind, but it's always occurring, regardless of what you're doing.

Mary also observes that while we tend to be ruled by our thoughts, most of the time this mental domination doesn't serve us very well. When we're absorbed in our thinking, we're "away" in our thoughts, "somewhere else," often in the past or the future. Much of what we think about doesn't turn out to be that useful because it's not related to real life and our world. The thinking mind is more like a machine that starts running and creates a world of its own.

The opposite of living in the world of our thoughts is being in the present, fully "here" and "now," with our thinking available to inform us but not running the show.

Mary calls us to question our relationship to our thinking, to notice ways it doesn't serve us and actually obstructs our wholeness. Because we've been indoctrinated to think a certain way and because that type of thinking is continually supported and reinforced by our culture, observing our thinking requires awareness. We're bucking the system by thinking outside the box.

The mass belief system largely promoted in our world today is founded on doubting anything other than data gleaned from physically based sources and conclusions based on agreed-upon forms of logical thinking. Clearly, this kind of process has its value and has allowed us to make all kinds of advances in understanding and dealing with our world. The problem is, we've been reduced to thinking that this is the only trustworthy source of information. This is a great loss because it excludes much of who we are: our subconscious input (gut feelings and instincts), our emotions and feelings, and information from the higher mind, such as intuition, psychic powers, telepathy, and connections with beings and dimensions that aren't physically manifest.

Mary explains that we've been convinced to limit ourselves to a mental box because it's made us easier to control. However, we have a choice about what we accept as true and the kind of input we open ourselves to receive. That is something our leaders and the people in control don't want us to know because this form of domination only works if we agree to think in the ways we've been taught. Once we realize we have a choice, we can choose something else. At the least, we can explore other possibilities and see if they provide more support for living the way we would like.

An incident that occurred a number of years ago in my life

showed me the importance of trusting my higher intuition. My partner and I had just begun developing an eighteen-acre parcel of forested land in Hawaii. We were hand-clearing a spot that was to become the parking area in the center of the property. As I was working, I suddenly began to feel ill, which seemed strange since I'd felt completely fine just minutes before. I continued working, and my discomfort continued to increase. At a certain point, I realized that the spirits of the land were causing my bodily symptoms; they were trying to tell me that we were making a mistake and shouldn't be clearing that place. I told my partner, but he didn't believe me and said we should just keep going. Because I trusted the message, I stood my ground. Finally, I convinced him that we should take fifteen minutes and see if there was another location that would be better for the parking area. In less than five minutes, we found a new place that we both immediately recognized was much more suitable. Once we decided to make the new place the parking area, my bodily symptoms completely vanished. It wasn't until much later, when we knew our property better, that we realized we'd gotten confused; we had thought the original area we were clearing was in the center of the property, but it was actually only a few feet away from the side border. The new location we had been guided to was almost exactly in the middle of the property.

How did I know that I was communicating with the spirits of the land? I can't really explain it. I just knew. It reminds me of a question I used to have when I was young: How do you know when you're in love? The answer I received was, "When it happens, you just know." Judging by the number of people who have had the experience of being in love, I think it's true that most of us know what it's like to just know something. This kind of knowing is what allows us to expand beyond the limits of the physical dimension, which includes connecting with beings in other dimensions.

Mary states unequivocally that she and many other higher beings are absolutely real and want to help us—and also that we ourselves are higher beings. The confidence with which she makes this statement is contagious: as I listen to her, I feel complete faith and peace in her statement. And her words resonate with my own experience. I've interacted with nonphysical beings—including Mary—and I've experienced my own higher self.

To release habits or mental blocks that interfere with our wholeness, the first step is to notice how we limit ourselves with our insecurity. Then we can make a conscious choice to open to all the parts of ourselves and our world. This will help us to transform restricting mental patterns such as habitual doubt of experiences that are beyond sensory input and logical thinking.

Another mental block to experiencing the entirety of our reality is the tendency for our lower minds to engage in continuous thought. Our nonstop thinking is like static from a radio that's always playing. It screens us from connecting with much of what's actually happening. To overcome this pattern, Mary recommends meditation, in which we learn to consciously turn off the lower mind. As she so beautifully expresses, being able to quiet our thoughts enables us to receive God's embrace because our lower mind is no longer blocking us.

Another way we can learn to relate to the world differently is by listening to the ideas of people who have overcome their mental blocks. Hearing perspectives that are more open will reinforce new, more spacious ways of thinking and challenge our conventional, limiting patterns. Listening to awakened teachers and reading spiritual literature are two avenues for doing this.

What I call spiritual transmission is a particularly powerful process that supports our opening to the greater reality. It occurs when the experience of higher consciousness is transferred from one person to another. Mary describes what spiritual transmission feels like: "your body opens, your mind relaxes, your heart is filled with love, and you experience the joy of greater connection to God."

The first time I glimpsed one of my spiritual teachers, I had a potent experience of spiritual transmission. He was just leaving a meditation session with some of his devotees at his retreat sanctuary in Northern California, and as I watched him, I was immediately struck by the incredible grace and beauty of his movements. He seemed to almost float above the ground, moving with the greatest ease I'd ever witnessed. This is saying a lot because I was a dancer with a highly developed eye for movement. Peace and freedom emanated from him, and all sense of time felt suspended for the next twenty or so seconds. I watched him proceed with apparent effortlessness to his home, where he seamlessly disappeared behind the gate. Afterward I felt bathed in joy, relieved of any concerns or heaviness, and filled with light.

As Mary points out, this kind of transmission can also occur through a gathering of people, such as a church group. It can happen through an empowered object or place, such as a crystal, a sacred artifact, or a sacred mountain or river. We can also experience spiritual transmission from beings who aren't physically manifest. I experience this through my connections with Mary and continue to experience it when I read her messages.

I find Mary's guidelines for exercising discernment to be valuable and accurate. Not every interaction with other beings or every idea that we encounter necessarily supports our highest good. This applies to interactions with physically manifest beings as well as to encounters with nonincarnate entities or energies. If we use the criteria that Mary suggests—our body opens, our mind relaxes, our heart is filled with love, and we experience the joy of greater connection to God—we can discern whether our experience supports our total well-being.

Once again, we have choice as to whether or not we open ourselves to any particular experience or point of view. Developing awareness of how we feel and what we experience within ourselves in response to various energies and thought forms can protect us. Through her guidelines, Mary provides us with a structure for maintaining our safety, one that supports us in making wise choices so that we don't need to block out all that is unfamiliar or new.

One aspect of developing discernment is to learn to differentiate the transmission of energy from any beliefs that are attached to it. One may feel supportive to us while the other doesn't. For example, sometimes people are drawn to the personal energy of a charismatic leader and then unquestioningly accept ideas that they would normally reject. Mary advises us to test the concepts being espoused to see if they resonate with our experience and to gauge how they affect our inner world. If the beliefs "open your body, relax your mind, fill your heart with love, and connect you with God," they are likely to be safe. If they support fear, separation, guilt, blame, or other such qualities, they are not to be trusted.

When I was a thirteen, my family visited the Mormon Tabernacle in Salt Lake City and participated in their program for introducing the public to their church. The program presented a well-produced movie that attractively portrayed Mormon beliefs, edifices, and beautiful music from the Mormon Tabernacle choir. I received a strong spiritual transmission and considered joining the church on the basis of my experience. However, when I considered the ideas they were promoting, I realized it wasn't a fit for me. My experience is an example of Mary's instructions: I was able to separate Mormon beliefs from the power of the transmission and realize that those beliefs didn't align with my values.

I greatly appreciate Mary's final communications in this message. She acknowledges the courage and strength it takes to go beyond mass beliefs and says that when we do so, other people may feel threatened. Although others may think they need us to share their beliefs, that's not actually necessary. We can love others without adopting their ideas, and we never support others by limiting ourselves. Our greatest support comes from engaging in action from our highest self, which may lead us to make choices that are different from others' choices but never limits our ability to love and be compassionate.

Mary closes by inviting all of us to join her and all the beings of light who are supporting and loving us in their blissful state:

> We invite you into the vast space of love and freedom in God that we enjoy. It is beautiful here. And you do not have to leave where you are to join us. But you will have to open your minds. Your doubt is limiting you. We do not ask you to believe anything. Simply let go of your doubt and notice what you experience. We are right here, and we love you profoundly.

A vast space of love and freedom sounds extremely attractive to me. It is not without work, but it is worth working for. I thank you, Mary, and all the beings of light you represent, for this wonderful offer.

EIGHT

The Nature of Reality

Beloved ~

Today, I would like to speak about an idea that many people hold relative to spirituality. This is the idea that the world is an illusion. Some spiritual teachers have expressed this idea as a way of trying to help others to awaken and evolve in their consciousness. Sometimes this idea is expressed as saying that your emotions are an illusion or the physical world is an illusion. These ideas have confused some of you, and so I want to clarify the nature of reality.

Those of you reading this are in a body in the physical world, with emotions and feelings and thoughts and energies that you experience. All of these are a reflection of your consciousness. Whatever level of consciousness you have attained will be reflected in your outer world, like a mirror reflects your image. Many people at this time are at a level of consciousness that is reflected in the third-dimensional reality, and this has been the case for a long time on Earth.

Now, at this time period, many people are beginning to grow and rise in their consciousness. Many are beginning to awaken to higher levels of consciousness. Some are experiencing the fourth dimension, fifth dimension, and even the sixth dimension. Most of you who are awakening to higher dimensions are not yet stably or fully seated or located there. Rather, you find yourself moving between the third dimension and the higher dimensions.

One reason so many are beginning to awaken at this time is that Earth herself is moving into higher-dimensional frequencies of the fourth dimension. This is releasing tremendous energies and support for human spiritual growth. There have always been some who were awakened to higher dimensions of consciousness. You called these your great realizers, teachers, mystics, saints, sages, and prophets. However, they were very few because it was quite difficult to attain this level and because Earth's energies weren't supporting this growth in the way that is happening now. So this is a very special time, and we are moving into a new age when many will attain higher consciousness.

When this occurs for an individual or for a group of people, the shift will be reflected in your outer reality. Whatever consciousness you hold will determine the form you experience in your outer reality. However, there is a subtle trick, you might say, to all this. And it is that you cannot merely think yourself into creating the kind of reality that you desire. It is not enough to understand with your mind that this is an illusion because your mind is not the same as your consciousness. Your mind is an instrument of separation, whereas your consciousness is a force of unity. Your consciousness includes all of who you are. It does not exclude anything. It doesn't exclude your body, your emotions and feelings, your energy, or your external reality.

If you try to think yourself into a higher realization, such as thinking that this is all an illusion, the result is that you will repress parts of your reality. And whatever is repressed will have power over you. Its natural power will simply be active and unimpeded, and since it is being repressed, that power will work to keep you stuck, fixed at the level you're currently at.

Your mind is not capable of growing you into a higher dimension. It is important to understand that consciousness is not the same as your mind. Consciousness includes all of who you are. The mind can support the process of transformation in consciousness, but it cannot direct it. Consciousness is greater than the mind.

The idea that this world is an illusion is a description of how the world will seem from a higher dimension, a higher level of consciousness. It will seem more dreamlike, more malleable, softer, more easily changeable or shifting, less fixed. Some teachers have used the analogy that when you are asleep, your dream world often seems completely real to you, but when you wake up you relate to it differently—as just a dream. These teachers have gone on to suggest that it is possible to awaken from the seeming reality of this world in a similar manner, and then it won't seem so real but more like an illusion.

There is truth to this, but it is something that is realized naturally as you grow into higher consciousness. This world will seem less fixed, rigid, constricting. At that higher level of consciousness, your energy is naturally drawn to other arenas through the natural process of the law of attraction. You are no longer operating primarily at the frequency levels that create the kind of world you experience now, so this kind of world will not be reflected in the mirror of your external circumstances.

The key in all this is to be aware that the shift in understanding relative to the nature of our reality is a result of a natural process of growth and transformation in consciousness. Being aware of this may help motivate you to engage the process that leads to transformation. It's like getting a glimpse or a picture of what's possible. But the glimpse or picture isn't sufficient, in most cases, to make it so.

In fact, this idea that the world is an illusion can be used in ways that thwart or obstruct the process of growth. It can be used as a means of denying what is, which is a way of denying your consciousness—since All That Is, is a reflection of your consciousness. And whatever is denied stays stuck in darkness, not available to the light.

The process that allows you to change and grow in consciousness is for you to receive God's light and to infuse it with love. And this must be done with all the aspects of consciousness. So receive God's light into your bodies and infuse it with love. Receive God's light into your emotions and feelings and infuse it with love. Receive God's light into your sexuality and infuse it with love. Receive God's light into all the "external" circumstances you encounter in your life and infuse it with love. This is the practice that will move you into the higher dimensions. And then, when you have attained that higher level of consciousness, it will be naturally obvious to you that the lower frequencies you were attracting or creating through your previous state of consciousness were limited compared to what you are now attracting and creating. And you will then see your old framework and assumptions about reality, the old way you related to reality, as a kind of illusion.

One way of thinking about this is to remember your perceptions of life as a child. When you were a child, you had a certain way of relating to life, certain ideas or perceptions. You might have thought of your parents as perfect or invincible or all-powerful. When you grew up, you realized that this was an illusion, and you understood those ideas differently and related to them differently. Your parents no longer had the power over you they once did because you had grown and changed. This didn't occur because, as a child, you told yourself that your relationship with your parents was an illusion. Your relationship with them was true at that time, given your level of development and awareness and sophistication. Once you grew and changed, however, it became obvious that the old ideas and form of relationship were a kind of illusion. You didn't bring about the change through changing your ideas. You changed your whole self naturally, organically, through your growth, and your ideas and thinking naturally changed as a part of that.

Trying to figure everything out can be a trap that distracts you from the actual process of growth that will reveal to you all you need to know. You can be fooled by your mind to think that you're being spiritual when you may simply be thinking about spirituality, which is different from living a spiritual life.

Do not use your thoughts to deny any parts of life. All life is to be loved and opened to the light. Let the light transform you. You do not need to do it from your mind or from any other limited part of yourself. Open yourself to light and the transformation will inevitably occur, and then the transformation will be reflected in your mind as well as in your world. This is the way it always happens.

And if you want to accelerate the change, bring your love to all the parts of yourself and your reality. Love is the great accelerator. Open to light, and charge the light with your love. It's that simple. All else will fall into place and align itself in God's perfect plan.

I love you and support you in this beautiful process.
I AM Mary Magdalene

I am in awe of the simplicity and directness with which Mary tackles such a complex topic as the illusory nature of our world. Her mastery and light shine through in a profound way in this communication.

She begins by acknowledging that the spiritual idea that this world is an illusion has confused some of us and moves on to discuss the nature of our reality. First, she describes what most of us currently experience: that we live in a physical world in bodies that have physical sensations, emotions, thoughts, and energies. She says that our experience of ourselves is a reflection of our consciousness. Right now, most of us are rooted in third-dimensional consciousness, and that's reflected in our world of physical manifestation.

I want to clarify the terms *consciousness* and *dimensions of reality* because these concepts are unfamiliar to some people and have been used to refer to various ideas. I define *consciousness* as our awareness of reality. In this sense, reality refers to ourselves as well as to all that exists around us. As we grow spiritually, our consciousness evolves and our perceptions of ourselves and our world change.

The states of consciousness attained as a result of spiritual growth are often referred to as *higher consciousness*. *Higher* is not a judgment but rather a description of an actual change in state. You might compare higher consciousness to higher education, where *higher* doesn't mean the education is better than previous forms of education. Rather, it's something that builds upon prior education, and thus *higher* refers to a developmental framework.

There are two aspects to our progression of consciousness: our spiritual growth alters our consciousness, and our consciousness creates our reality. Thus, as we grow, we create a different reality. The various states of reality are called dimensions, and each dimension correlates to a different form of consciousness. We tend to be most familiar with the third dimension because that's the dimension (and the consciousness) most of us primarily abide in at this time.

I use a schema, or what I call a map of consciousness, to help in understanding the progression of our conscious evolution. It contains twelve dimensions. As you read this, please keep in mind that any given dimension includes awareness of all lower dimensions.

The first dimension—the mineral kingdom—is made up of atoms, subatomic particles, and molecules: it contains the building blocks of all form. While there isn't self-awareness in this dimension, there is a basic kind of consciousness. Shamans call upon the spirits of the mineral kingdom—air, fire, water, and earth—as part of sacred ceremony. Crystals, which are part of the mineral kingdom, are believed to be conduits of spiritual power. And some people believe the codes in our DNA belong to the first dimension.

The second dimension consists of biological matter that comprises the plant and lower animal kingdoms. In this dimension, there is awareness of species and species subgroups, such as herds, and also an awareness of needs for food, protection, aggression, and procreation. Consciousness at this level is largely instinctual and is focused on survival and the present moment. A form of consciousness exists in this dimension that responds to care. For example, plants respond when given loving care. The second dimension is present in humans through our autonomic nervous system, which regulates our life-support functions and our instinctive responses to life.

The third dimension, which includes the higher animal kingdom and humans, is where beings first become aware of themselves as individual souls. This is generally experienced as a sense of separation from all else. There is awareness of time—in terms of past, present, and future—as well as awareness of cause and effect. Beings at this level become conscious of having individual choice and the power to determine their circumstances. They also become aware of their effect on others and can choose to be responsible (response-able) to others. While the primary focus in the third dimension continues to be on the physical plane, there is awareness of feelings and thoughts in the third dimension. In particular, this level is characterized by dualistic thinking, in which experience is interpreted in terms of opposites: good/bad, right/wrong, light/dark, energy/matter, life/death, pleasure/pain, love/hate, and so forth.

The dimensions above the third dimension are often referred to as the "higher dimensions" since the majority of humans are still operating within the context of the third dimension. However, as Mary points out,

> Now, at this time period, many people are beginning to… awaken to higher levels of consciousness. Some are experiencing the fourth dimension, fifth dimension, and even the sixth dimension. Most of you who are awakening to higher dimensions are not yet stably or fully seated or located there. Rather, you find yourself moving between the third dimension and the higher dimensions.

The first of these higher dimensions, the fourth dimension, is sometimes referred to as the astral plane. In this dimension, we still experience ourselves as individuals in a world of duality, but our world is much more mutable. We're now aware that our thoughts and feelings create our reality. The laws of time and space are quite fluid, similar to what we experience in our dreams. And like dreams, things can change quickly here.

Because the astral plane is an emotionally based dimension, a person's level of emotional mastery will determine which parts of the astral dimension they will experience. The lower astral plane, ruled by fear and sorrow, is where we experience nightmares and is often portrayed as hell or the hell-realms. The higher astral plane, characterized by love, is where we experience happiness, harmony, and the higher vibrations that eventually lead us to even higher dimensions. Mary's focus on our need to learn to respond to painful feelings is aimed at helping us master this emotional plane and move on to the higher realms.

It's in the fourth dimension that we become aware of our six bodies: the physical, etheric, emotional, mental, causal, and spiritual

Figure 8-1. MAP OF CONSCIOUSNESS

Supreme Creator
Undifferentiated Oneness

12th Dimension
MOTHER-FATHER GOD
I AM PRESENCE

8th – 11th Dimensions
SOUL GROUPS, ANGELS,
ASCENDED MASTERS

7th Dimension
LUMINOUS BEINGS OF LIGHT
IN SERVICE TO LIFE

6th Dimension
MAGICAL AND BLESSED LIFE
DIRECTED BY SPIRIT

5th Dimension
UNITY CONSCIOUSNESS:
UNCONDITIONAL LOVE AND ACCEPTANCE

4th Dimension
ASTRAL PLANE:
EMOTIONALLY BASED AND DREAMLIKE

3rd Dimension
HIGHER ANIMAL KINGDOM AND HUMANS:
SEPARATION AND DUALITY

2nd Dimension
PLANT AND LOWER ANIMAL KINGDOM:
SPECIES/HERD CONSCIOUSNESS

1st Dimension
MINERAL KINGDOM AND ELEMENTAL SPIRITS:
RUDIMENTARY CONSCIOUSNESS

bodies. The etheric (energy) body acts as an interface between the physical and our other bodies. The emotional body, or astral body, is where we learn emotional mastery, which includes abilities for advanced dreaming, imagination, psychic powers, intuition, magic, and creativity. The mental body is the domain of mastery of our thoughts and the ability to consciously create our reality. The causal body is the source of our sense of self, our conscience, and the record of our soul's journey through time. Our spiritual body contains our I AM presence, which is our individualized connection to the Supreme Creator as well as the link to the higher dimensions.

Some people are born with a high degree of awareness of the astral realm. These individuals may find it hard to relate to the third-dimensional, physically based realm and may need to consciously develop that ability. Others who are physically oriented may not have a natural, or already-developed, connection to the astral plane. These people often discount the higher-frequency realms beyond the physical as "woo-woo" or unreal.

The teachings that suggest that the world is an illusion can be understood as a means to shake up the thinking that denies any reality other than the physically based, third-dimensional reality. But it's also a description of actual experience in the higher realms. Beginning with the fourth dimension and continuing beyond, physical reality becomes less and less prominent and fixed, until eventually we go beyond it altogether—although the choice to manifest physically still remains an option.

The real illusion is *our relationship* to the third-dimensional reality. It's an illusion that our world is as fixed and solid as it seems. This concept was brought home for me when I was in my early twenties and had a conversation with a Chinese physician about different ways to relate to the physical world. Using the example of malaria, the doctor was illustrating how Chinese medicine works. In Western medicine, he told me, the view is that malaria is caused by a germ that mosquitoes carry, and it's treated with medications that kill the germ. By contrast, Chinese medicine sees malaria as an imbalance in the body's energy system and heals the disease by restoring balance through acupuncture and herbs. He then affirmed that both systems are effective in curing malaria. The choice of which treatment to use and how successful it is generally depends on which modality the patient believes in. His simple explanation helped me to see that my physically based presumptions about how the world operates may be limited—or perhaps not accurate at all.

As we stabilize in higher-dimensional consciousness, it will become increasingly clear that the world isn't necessarily operating in the concrete, material way we previously thought. However, prior to that time, there's an implicit danger in holding onto the idea that the world is an illusion. Some people interpret the concept of *illusion* as meaning that we don't have to do anything relative to our physical, emotional, and etheric bodies other than remind ourselves that they're not real, because they don't actually exist. While our relationship to our bodies, emotions, and energy is vastly different in the higher dimensions, that isn't our reality in the third and fourth dimensions. If we're manifesting in the third and fourth dimensions, we have practical, spiritual work to do in order to purify these bodies. Eventually, this work will free our energy and consciousness to manifest at a higher level, but until then merely thinking that this world is unreal won't be enough to move us beyond the lower dimensions. In fact, that thinking may divert us from doing the work that *would* move us forward by convincing us it's unnecessary. In that case, we end up with a kind of split personality, where our mental body projects—to the best of its ability—the belief that the third-dimensional reality is unreal, while our physical, emotional, and etheric bodies are stuck in third- and lower fourth-dimensional patterns.

I've seen this kind of split occur in relation to the idea of fearless-ness, which is held by many as a superior spiritual state to be attained. When I hear people claim to be fearless or promoting the non-necessity of fear, I often suspect that they're afraid of feeling fear. While the *idea* of being fearless may be consoling, it doesn't actually change the fear. In fact, the idea tends to hide both the actual feeling and the path of transformation. If they were to do the work of trans-forming their fear, they would eventually arrive at a state of fearless-ness, but it would be a state of total being rather than merely an ideal.

The idea that this world is an illusion can be helpful as a seed thought that motivates us to grow beyond our present reality. It also can be one possible tool for gaining mastery of our mental body and bringing us to a state of receptivity for higher ways to relate to arising phenomena. However, this idea needs to be held in balance with the larger objective of working with *all* the bodies in the fourth dimension. This includes engaging the physical, emotional, and etheric realms until we have truly mastered and moved beyond our current reality.

Sometimes, people have opened up to me about a challenge or emotional disturbance only to suddenly remind themselves that it isn't real and abruptly end the conversation. In those instances, I had been feeling a strong connection to the person's experience and emo-tions until they announced it wasn't real; at that point I suddenly felt a void, as if a door were closing. When that happens, I feel con-cerned that the idea of the world being unreal is being used to deny and suppress what is actually very real.

We need to be able to discern the difference between denial or suppression and actual transcendence. The faculty of feeling is the instrument for that discernment. When someone has truly moved to a higher dimension, you feel from them an increase in light and love. But when a person is merely projecting the thoughts of a higher-dimensional reality, you feel an absence or decrease in light and love, often along with tension or a kind of emptiness from suppressing their life force. Developing this ability to discern feelings is part of developing our mastery in the fourth dimension.

I want to briefly describe the fifth, sixth, and seventh dimensions, as I understand them. In the fifth dimension, we've gone beyond the sense of separation or limitation. While we still manifest as individual beings, we live in unity consciousness in Spirit, constantly experiencing the oneness of Mother-Father God/All That Is. Beings in this dimension have realized unconditional love, unconditional forgiveness, and unconditional acceptance. They have transcended space and time, leaving only the here and now of being. Fifth-dimensional beings instantly manifest whatever they want, and their desires are always in harmony with the will of the Creator. Suffering and pain are no longer required to learn lessons in this realm. Instead of carbon-based, physical bodies that experience physical suffering, fifth-dimensional beings have crystalline-based bodies that do not age or deteriorate. These beings don't experience judgment, guilt, or negativity. Rather than polarizing the world into opposites, they see all qualities as unified aspects of a single whole. The fifth dimension is probably what most people imagine when they think of heaven.

The sixth and seventh dimensions are still associated with individual consciousness, but the beings at these levels are increasingly light-based and operate at higher frequencies. In the sixth dimension, all of life is seen as magical and blessed. Every aspect of life is directed and advanced through the work of Spirit, while individuals still exercise their abilities as creators. The morphogenic field that connects all beings and things is obvious at this level. Through portals, sixth-dimensional beings are able to time travel, travel between parallel lives, and travel to other places in the universe. The sixth dimension reveals the beautiful and intricate pattern of the universe, a pattern that forms the foundation for sacred geometry and music.

In the seventh dimension, individuation takes the form of luminous light beings who are fully aware of their mission in Spirit. Beings in this dimension carry higher consciousness to others on a large scale, through teaching and healing or by transmitting energy through their auras so that others can access it.

The dimensions beyond the seventh are planes of soul groups or oversouls, which include angelic groups, extraterrestrials, and groups of beings of light. At these higher dimensions, beings are progressively responsible for Earth, our solar system, our galaxy, and our universe. The twelfth, or highest, dimension is the domain of our Mother-Father God and the origin of our I AM presence. Beyond that is the undifferentiated Source of All: the Supreme Creator, or Absolute Oneness.

While I think it's useful to understand the full map—at least in very basic form—at our present stage of spiritual development, most of us are growing beyond the third and lower fourth dimensions into the higher fourth and fifth dimensions. The fourth dimension is often viewed as a transitional dimension from the third into the fifth. The mastery of our four lower bodies—physical, etheric, emotional, and mental—occurs in the fourth dimension, and we complete our life lessons in the third and fourth dimensions: this work allows us to reside on a stable basis in the fifth dimension.

In the past, the rare beings who were able to awaken to higher dimensions were often referred to as masters, saints, mystics, sages, realizers, and great teachers. The large number of people who are currently awakening signifies a unique period in our history. Mary gives two reasons for this shift. The first is that Earth herself is moving into the fourth dimension. Earth isn't just an inert mass of atoms and molecules: rather, she's a living, sentient being, the Divine Mother in one of her forms of manifestation—a very powerful form for those of us on this planet. This movement of Earth from a third- to fourth-dimensional being is supporting all beings on Earth in advancing spiritually along with her.

Mary alludes to a second reason why so many people are awakening at this time: in the past very few awakened because it was quite difficult to attain this level. Here, Mary refers to what some other channeled beings and entities call a "divine dispensation." At this time, we've been given a special allowance that alters the previous requirement that beings purify *all* of their karma before moving into the fifth dimension. Purifying our karma is an enormous endeavor that includes releasing the effects of past actions through self-responsibility, cleansing actions, forgiveness, and love. It includes completing one's soul lessons in any given arena. It also includes becoming free of attachment to experience in a particular area—and ultimately in all areas—by becoming more grounded in the love and light of God, which is prior to, and not dependent upon, experience.

Some channeled beings tell us that because of the divine dispensation in effect at this time, we now need only purify fifty-one percent of our karma and master our four lower bodies in order to move into the fifth dimension. Mary confirms this, calling the present "a very special time" in which many people will attain higher consciousness. I find this tremendously exciting, and I also feel greatly blessed to be alive and here on Earth at this time. While I have been a dedicated spiritual practitioner my whole life, I feel even more motivated to engage my spirituality because of the powerful energies and opportunities for growth we are blessed with right now.

Part of our process of growth into the higher dimensions is learning to differentiate between thinking and consciousness. Mary astutely points out that thinking creates separation, whereas consciousness is a force of unity that encompasses all of who we are. If our thinking negates any aspect of us or our reality, it constricts our consciousness. As she points out, anything we repress will gain power over us in our unconscious and become a barrier to our growth.

Mary offers a description of how we'll experience the world in the higher dimensions, saying that it will seem "more dreamlike, more malleable, softer, more easily changeable or shifting, less fixed." Like the idea that the world is an illusion, this glimpse of what's possible can inspire us to grow and give us direction for that growth. Nonetheless, she reminds us that, in most cases, the glimpse isn't sufficient to make it so.

This comment of Mary's reminds me of a phenomenon I observed when I was in a spiritual community led by a guru. The guru would offer occasions of meditation or eye-gazing with the devotees, and people would have remarkable spiritual experiences. Yet, these experiences themselves generally weren't sufficient to bring about lasting change unless they were accompanied by ongoing spiritual practice. It's easy to become attached, or you might even say addicted, to spiritual experiences and use them as an alternative to engaging in the work of further transformation. In such cases, the experiences distract and divert us from our growth process.

What does make transformation possible? Mary tells us clearly. We must receive God's light into our bodies, emotions, feelings, and sexuality and infuse it with love. We must receive God's light into all the circumstances we encounter in life and infuse it with love. When we are able to do this, Mary assures us, we will see all of our old assumptions about reality as a kind of illusion.

There is another way of deluding ourselves that Mary warns us about it. We can easily believe we're being spiritual when we're only *thinking about* spiritual ideas. One of my teachers used to call this being an "armchair spiritual practitioner."

Mary tells us we do not need to create transformation from our minds or from any other limited part of ourselves. If we open ourselves to light, the transformation will inevitably occur and will be reflected in our minds as well as in our world. This instruction creates a shift from the idea that we are doing a particular spiritual practice that is transforming us. Rather, we are doing things that are opening us to the light, and the light is what is transforming us. She tells us that it always happens this way.

As I listen to Mary's final paragraph, I am again transported into the beauty of which she speaks. And so I close this commentary with her completing sentences, which carry me beyond words into ecstasy:

> And if you want to accelerate the process, bring your love to all the parts of yourself and your reality. Love is the great accelerator. Open to light, and charge the light with your love. It's that simple. All else will fall into place and align itself in God's perfect plan.

NINE

The Work for Men—and Many Women, Too

Dear ones ~

Many of you have heard that this is a time when the Feminine is coming to the fore to lead the way. This is so and must be if we are to move through the birth canal we are presently in and into the new age before us. Many of you also wonder what this means for men. How are they to participate and support this change? And so I would like to speak to this.

Some of the work for men at this time is to bring forth their inner Feminine. There are two primary arenas of this work. The first is in reconnecting with their emotions. For a long time, men have been trained since their youngest years to repress and deny their emotions, especially the emotions of fear and sadness. This has caused great harm to men and to the world. When energy is repressed, it doesn't just vanish—it always goes somewhere. In the case of emotions that are repressed, the energy generally shows up as aggression and violence toward others or as physical illness. Another way of saying this is that the energy either moves outward, as aggression toward others, or inward, as illness, depression, or shame. Individuals, and the world altogether, have suffered these negative symptoms for far too long. It is high time to heal these negative effects of emotional repression and to change the patterns at their source.

This means that men must learn to allow their emotions. They must reengage their feeling nature so that they have the ability to feel their emotions fully. They must set aside the mechanisms they've learned that make them deny and doubt their feelings. They must retrain the mind to be a partner with their feeling nature, rather than a dominator and jailor. This is a great work for men and also for many women who have been similarly trained in the Masculine-dominated mode of denying their feelings, which has been the mode of your world for so long. It is helpful to get support in this, as it is such a deeply ingrained pattern to repress and deny your feeling nature. Groups such as The Mankind Project and Nonviolent Communication are supporting individuals in making this shift. As I have said before, remembering and reconnecting with your feeling nature is essential for opening the heart. And it is a major area of work for many people at this time, especially men, as a prerequisite for growth in the higher spiritual realms.

Some of you have emotional wounds from the past that have not yet been healed. You survived these traumas by separating from them—either emotionally, mentally, or physically. You built a kind of psychic wall or enclosure around them so that you could get on with your life and so that the incidents would not pull you down or even sink you in the overwhelming depth and pain you were experiencing in those events. These places within yourself also need to be healed, for your energy is bound and trapped in these places and is not free for your spiritual growth. You may need help for this healing work, through a counselor or guide, and you should seek this help, as it is important that these traumas be healed and the trapped energy be released.

The other area that men need to focus on to support their Feminine to come to the fore is development of their ability to be inclusive. And this, too, applies to women who are not developed in this area and have been trained predominantly in the masculine mode of competition. This means that you must learn to be as sensitive to others as you are to yourselves, as caring about their needs getting met as you are about your own. It is a major shift into abundance consciousness, as to do this means that you are trusting that there is enough for everyone. Competition is based upon the assumption of lack: there isn't enough for everyone and, therefore, some will be the winners and get what they need or desire and others won't.

There actually *is* enough for everyone, but to realize this requires a grand shift in consciousness. It is part of the shift that you are undergoing at this time. You will realize this abundance when you make the shift. And to make the shift, you must assume this abundance. So it takes trust, or you might call it faith, to do this. Ultimately, the abundance is in the divine realm, where there is infinite abundance. You must link up with the Divine, tap into that ultimate source of abundance, and then you will have the ability to shift into abundance consciousness.

When you think about abundance, many of you envision financial abundance or an abundance of the things in your life that you desire. This is one form of abundance, but it is not the greatest form. That is why I like the term *inclusiveness*, because it helps you to envision other forms of abundance.

Babies assume complete abundance. They assume that all of their needs will get met. A baby doesn't think, "Well, there isn't enough milk now for me, so I should just stay quiet and not cry, even though I'm hungry. Or maybe I can take my brother's food, and then I'll have enough." Babies assume that their needs will get met, and they always communicate those needs, which is their form of asking to receive—usually in ways that immediately get our attention! So the first form of abundance is with yourself—assuming there is enough for you to have what you need. Our ultimate need, our ultimate food, is love. And there is always enough of that.

Now you are an adult and are not like a baby whose needs are taken care of by its parents. Now you need to give to yourself, be the parent for yourself. So you begin by including all parts of yourself, by caring for yourself like a loving parent, by inviting back any part of you that has been excluded, ignored, or repressed.

If young children have been well loved and provided for, it is natural for them to begin to expand this caring and loving into their sphere of relations. It will first extend to their parents and family, later to their friends, teachers, classmates, and neighbors. Eventually, it will be a form of relating to all people. This is a natural progression of human development. However, if the Feminine is being suppressed, if the idea has been instilled that there isn't enough for everyone, that it's me versus you, winners and losers, then this progression gets interfered with. Then we end up with adults who are self-focused without the balance of awareness and caring about others. It's like having emotional blinders on.

When you have a conversation, are you aware of the others involved as well as yourself? Are you connected to them, listening to them, noticing their response to your sharing? Is everyone included in the conversation, or is it dominated by one person? Are you giving as much time and attention to the ones who are quiet or less verbal as you are to the ones who are quick to respond and have much to say? Are you respecting others' opinions and choices, even when they're different from yours?

When you engage intimately with a partner, are you sensing their level of interest and response as well as your own? Are you making space for them to initiate as well as you? Are you giving to them for the pure joy of contributing to their pleasure and not because you're hoping or expecting that it will produce a desired outcome of your design? Are you waiting to be met by them in their energy level and interest so that you create the moment together, rather than leading with your own agenda? Are you open to surrendering your own trajectory so that, out of the mystery of the present moment, you can create a mutual one with your partner?

This does not require that you give up your own desires and needs. What you're giving up is your clinging to these to the exclusion of others. It's the exclusion that you're giving up. You can care for yourself and love yourself while also caring for and loving others. Indeed, as you become strong in caring for and loving yourself, you will notice that when you truly care for yourself and love yourself, you inevitably include others. To care for ourselves and love ourselves, we must open our feeling nature and our awareness. When we have that openness, we not only feel and are aware of ourselves, but that same feeling and awareness naturally expands out toward others, and it becomes natural to include them in our caring and loving.

This inclusiveness will change your life. It will also change your world. And it is time for this change. Ultimately, it will lead you to God, as God includes all. And God is the source of all abundance. All is given from God. God is the All, and sharing that with all is the greatest joy.

I love you and bless you to enjoy this great abundance of God.
I AM Mary Magdalene

*M*ary is very aware of the confusion many are feeling about men's role during this period of change. In this communication, she points to two primary arenas in which men are called to support the strengthening of the Feminine: these are connecting with emotions and developing the ability to be inclusive. Both tasks involve shifts in consciousness, followed by changes in action that champion and free the inner Feminine. Since we live in a culture that so strongly favors and rewards the Masculine, these communications apply not only to men but also to women who have a dominant inner Masculine—which means many women.

Mary first points to men's need to reconnect with their emotions. Many men have been bombarded since they were very young with messages encouraging them to deny and repress their emotions: "Don't be a crybaby," "Don't be a scaredy-cat," "Don't be a sissy," "Be strong like a man" . . . There is an assumption behind this kind of indoctrination: that feeling emotions—particularly sadness and fear—is equivalent to being weak. Boys are trained to be tough (unfeeling) in the belief that this will make them stronger, better able to survive, more competent, and more attractive to the opposite sex.

I received this kind of indoctrination growing up. Even though our family consisted of three daughters, we were raised to deny and suppress our emotions in the style typical of the Masculine-oriented culture of that time. I didn't see my parents express sadness or fear, and I was generally punished or ridiculed for displaying these emotions, or simply guided to suppress them: "Don't cry," "It's OK," "Don't worry." I quickly adapted to our family's messages, learning that the only acceptable emotions were happiness and anger—and anger was only OK if you were an adult. Children were supposed to be happy. Period.

As a result, I learned to funnel my sadness and fear into forms of anger, and then I did my best to hide my anger. This led to many problems. Controlling and repressing my emotional energy created tremendous tension, which eventually manifested as debilitating headaches. Then, when I couldn't hold all that energy back any longer, it would erupt in outbursts of anger. Needless to say, I've suffered a great deal from the results of both of these patterns. Happily, I've experienced much healing through understanding that these problems were caused by emotional suppression, and by learning to embrace my emotions.

Emotional energy doesn't just vanish when it's suppressed; it always goes somewhere. In my case, the energy went into a physical ailment and a damaging relational pattern of discharging anger toward others. As Mary says, the energy either gets directed outward as aggression or violence—I often picture this as a volcano exploding or as a large fire hose directed toward others full force—or it gets directed inward as illness, shame, and depression. The destructiveness of this energy isn't due to emotions being bad or dangerous, as many of us have been taught; it's due to directing our emotional energy in unhealthy and counterproductive ways, mostly through suppressing our emotions or projecting them onto other people.

The antidote for this suppression or projection is learning to allow our emotions. As Mary clearly states, all people—men and women—who have learned to habitually suppress emotions must reengage their ability to feel their emotions fully, setting aside the mechanisms that make them deny and doubt their feelings. The mind must be retrained to be a partner with their feeling nature, not a dominator or jailor.

I had to learn to cry as part of my retraining. For most of my adult life, I never cried. On the very rare occasions when I felt sadness or grief, I experienced it as a lump in my throat, but it never went further than that. A counselor was able to guide me in the process of remembering how to cry. First, she encouraged me to act like I was crying, mimicking the sounds, body gestures, and breathing that accompany crying. I began to look for times when I might be feeling sad. Since I didn't feel my sadness, I had to use my mind

Figure 9-1. LIST OF FEELINGS

These two charts come from the Center for Nonviolent Communication.
They contain an excellent list of our feelings, which lead us to our inner divine qualities.

Feelings Inventory

The following are words we use when we want to express a combination of emotional states and physical sensations. This list is neither exhaustive nor definitive. It is meant as a starting place to support anyone who wishes to engage in a process of deepening self-discovery and to facilitate greater understanding and connection between people.

There are two parts to this list: feelings we may have when our needs are being met and feelings we may have when our needs are not being met.

Feelings When Your Needs Are Satisfied

AFFECTIONATE
compassionate
friendly
loving
open-hearted
sympathetic
tender
warm

ENGAGED
absorbed
alert
curious
engrossed
enchanted
entranced
fascinated
interested
intrigued
involved
spellbound
stimulated

HOPEFUL
expectant
encouraged
optimistic

JOYFUL
amused
delighted
glad
happy
jubilant
pleased
tickled

EXCITED
amazed
animated
ardent
aroused
astonished
dazzled
eager
energetic
enthusiastic
giddy
invigorated
lively
passionate
surprised
vibrant

GRATEFUL
appreciative
moved
thankful
touched

INSPIRED
amazed
awed
wonder

CONFIDENT
empowered
open
proud
safe
secure

EXHILARATED
blissful
ecstatic
elated
enthralled
exuberant
radiant
rapturous
thrilled

PEACEFUL
calm
clear headed
comfortable
centered
content
equanimous
fulfilled
mellow
quiet
relaxed
relieved
satisfied
serene
still
tranquil
trusting

REFRESHED
enlivened
rejuvenated
renewed
rested
restored
revived

Feelings When Your Needs Are Not Satisfied

FATIGUE
beat
burnt out
depleted
exhausted
lethargic
listless
sleepy
tired
weary
worn out

ANNOYED
aggravated
dismayed
disgruntled
displeased
exasperated
frustrated
impatient
irritated
irked

ANGRY
enraged
furious
incensed
indignant
irate
livid
outraged
resentful

AVERSION
animosity
appalled
contempt
disgusted
dislike
hate
horrified
hostile
repulsed

CONFUSED
ambivalent
baffled
bewildered
dazed
hesitant
lost
mystified
perplexed
puzzled
torn

DISCONNECTED
alienated
aloof
apathetic
bored
cold
detached
distant
distracted
indifferent
numb
removed
uninterested
withdrawn

VULNERABLE
fragile
guarded
helpless
insecure
leery
reserved
sensitive
shaky

EMBARRASSED
ashamed
chagrined
flustered
guilty
mortified
self-conscious

AFRAID
apprehensive
dread
foreboding
frightened
mistrustful
panicked
petrified
scared
suspicious
terrified
wary
worried

PAIN
agony
anguished
bereaved
devastated
grief
heartbroken
hurt
lonely
miserable
regretful
remorseful

SAD
depressed
dejected
despair
despondent
disappointed
discouraged
disheartened
forlorn
gloomy
heavy hearted
hopeless
melancholy
unhappy
wretched

TENSE
anxious
cranky
distressed
distraught
edgy
fidgety
frazzled
irritable
jittery
nervous
overwhelmed
restless
stressed out

YEARNING
envious
jealous
longing
nostalgic
pining
wistful

DISQUIET
agitated
alarmed
discombobulated
disconcerted
disturbed
perturbed
rattled
restless
shocked
startled
surprised
troubled
turbulent
turmoil
uncomfortable
uneasy
unnerved
unsettled
upset

to guess when I was experiencing sadness. At those times, I engaged my pretend crying. Eventually, and sooner than I expected, the floodgates opened. At first, my tears were a trickle, but the trickle grew over time and eventually I was able to cry for real. To my surprise, I discovered that crying felt good! After I cried, I felt cleansed and released; the experience was like enjoying a rainbow after the storm. I no longer felt shame about crying. Instead, I experienced relief—and a kind of celebration in the growth that being able to cry signified for me.

I found it more challenging to reconnect with fear. I've made some progress, but it's still difficult for me to directly feel my fear; my deeply held pattern is to direct fear outward as anger. When I find myself getting angry now, however, I'm aware that it's most often a form of masked fear. Once I connect with the fear that's underneath the anger, I'm able to engage the process Mary recommends of responding to painful emotions. I have found that a natural process of release ensues. It is a natural, organic process that comes not because I've somehow gotten rid of the fear, but because the fear has completed its work. Fear, like any emotion, is simply a communication from one of my inner divine qualities that tells me something needs my attention. Once I connect with that inner divine quality, the emotion no longer needs to sounds its alert, and so it naturally resolves itself. I believe this is how emotions are designed to function.

I've helped many men and women reconnect with their emotions. I always emphasize that emotions aren't some kind of flaw in humans that merely makes extra work and causes discomfort. Emotions serve a crucial function by connecting us with our inner divine qualities so that we can attend to those qualities. Emotions are part of our body's amazing monitoring system; they help us stay on track, regain balance, and take care of ourselves. When we cut ourselves off from our emotions, we risk losing touch with our needs, which means we can't appropriately care for ourselves. Contrary to the popular notion that emotions make us weak, I see emotions as keeping us strong.

Mary discusses an even deeper function of emotions. Not only do they keep us healthy and able to care for ourselves, but when we let our emotions lead us to our inner divine qualities, our hearts open and we become loving, compassionate, spiritually connected beings. I think of our inner divine qualities as a bridge to God; our emotions lead us to that bridge. When we've reconnected with the inner divine qualities—the source of our feelings—we're on the bridge. By then, our feelings have served their purpose, so they naturally recede and subside. As our inner divine qualities shepherd us to reunite with our indwelling Divine, we cross over the bridge to "the other side."

Many of us survived painful emotional wounds in the past by disconnecting from our emotions and building a psychic fortress around them. When we reopen to our feelings, we begin to dismantle the fortresses, and our old wounds will, at some point, resurface for healing. Mary suggests that we may want to get help healing these wounds from a counselor or guide. This healing will free up blocks that impede our spiritual growth.

The second arena of growth for many men—as well as women with an underdeveloped inner Feminine—is the ability to be inclusive. Being inclusive involves developing sensitivity to ourselves but also to others—seeing their needs and giving them the same value and importance that we give our own. Others' needs aren't more important or less important; they're *equally* important. Inclusivity contrasts with the disposition of competition, which is a kind of me-first or me-at-all costs mentality. Inclusivity also contrasts to the you-first or you-at-all-costs attitude of martyrdom. Both competition and martyrdom are based on the idea of deficiency or lack, in which we feel there is not enough to meet everyone's needs. Mary insists that this fear of lack isn't necessary: in fact, there is enough for everyone to be included and to have their needs met.

I see the shift to an attitude of inclusivity as a major change of consciousness for humanity at this time. Making this change involves the assumption of *enoughness* or abundance for everyone, as well as a commitment to sharing the abundance so that everyone's needs are met. I sometimes refer to this as the family model. If a family gets some food—or any other resource—it's shared with all members of the family according to each one's need. Mary suggests that we relate to everyone in this way.

In the past, I've thought of abundance as an isolated, individual occurrence; abundance would allow me, as an individual, to have enough of the things I need and desire. Mary's concept of abundance is much bigger: the abundance she speaks of includes everyone. She tells us she likes the term *inclusiveness* because it points to this grand-scale abundance for all. Abundance isn't primarily about finances or an abundance of things, though it may include that; the greatest form of abundance "is in the divine realm, where there is infinite abundance." Clearly, to know true and ultimate abundance, we must unite with the Divine.

Mary gives the example of a baby as a being who assumes complete abundance to meet its needs. I find this example easy to relate to. We've all heard babies express their needs loudly and without hesitation, signaling how naturally they assume their needs will get met. At one time, we were all that way; we all assumed that enough resources were available to speedily and thoroughly satisfy our needs.

Now that we're adults, it's *our* job to attend to our needs, just as a parent attends to a baby. When we pay careful attention to our needs and generously practice self-care, our awareness inevitably

THE WORK FOR MEN—AND MANY WOMEN, TOO ⟶ 135

moves to caring about others and their needs. Through this natural progression we become adults founded in inclusiveness. However, if we haven't experienced receiving the care we need, from ourselves or from others, we tend to feel there isn't enough, and we become driven to compete for what we perceive as limited resources. The result is chronic anxiety over resources, as well as great tension as we try to acquire those resources.

Mary suggests that one way to measure our level of inclusiveness is to examine our conversations with others and look at how we interact in our intimate relationships. If we're dominating in the way we relate to others—unaware of their participation and responses or unwilling to share the lead, respect all, and cocreate the conversation or intimate engagement—we're probably not operating out of inclusiveness. Once again, Mary's mastery inspires and delights me as she uses these two commonplace situations to illustrate a somewhat elusive concept.

Returning to the idea that becoming inclusive doesn't mean giving up our own desires, Mary reminds us that we are not in an either-or, me-versus-you situation: there is enough for everyone. However, spiritually oriented people often think that it's not only necessary but also loftier to deny oneself in the service of others. Mary clarifies that inclusiveness means giving up the idea that it's necessary to exclude the needs of *anyone*—either our own or those of others. Yet, in practical application, inclusiveness requires that we love and give to ourselves first so that we have excess for loving others or giving to others. Think of the airline steward instructing parents to put on their oxygen masks before assisting their children. Obviously, we won't have anything to give if we haven't first taken care of ourselves. While this is apparent at an intellectual level, many of us still find it difficult to put ourselves first because of our training that we should take care of *others* instead of ourselves.

Mary closes this transmission by telling us what will happen if we start living out of inclusiveness and abundance. And once more, Mary's words lead me to God. Like the familiar expression, "All roads lead to Rome," with Mary, I find that all her words lead to God. And so I close again with her words, which consistently transport me to peace and joy:

> This inclusiveness will change your life. It will also change your world. And it is time for this change. Ultimately it will lead you to God, as God includes all. And God is the source of all abundance. All is given from God. God is the All, and sharing that with all is the greatest joy.

TEN

The Two Faces of God

Dear ones ~

I would like to speak of love. It has been said that God is love, and I agree with this. Love is also a path to God. And the most important part of that path is receiving God's love, opening your heart to God. When you open your heart, you always receive God's love because God's love is ever present. So the real process is about opening your heart.

And it's natural to have an open heart. What's unnatural is to have a closed heart. Some of you have closed your hearts because you've experienced pain and didn't know how to go through that pain and keep your heart open. Perhaps you experienced pain as a very young child and weren't helped by elders who had the wisdom to guide you in releasing and healing the pain. So you protected yourself by shutting down your heart.

Some people shut down their hearts as adults. This, too, is from pain. Perhaps you were hurt by someone you loved or experienced pain from the loss of a loved one. Or perhaps you went through a particularly painful life experience. And to protect yourself, you shut down your heart. This is an instinctive response of protection. It may serve you initially to get through a trauma, but if it becomes

137

an ongoing state, it doesn't serve you. It shuts you down; it closes you off from life, from your own heart.

Pain actually grows your heart. It deepens you, makes you more compassionate, more open. It's like the Grand Canyon, which was formed by the river wearing away the rock. The process brought out the beauty that was hidden before, that was only there in potential. And so it is with pain. It's part of the process of life at the third-dimensional level; it serves us, yet it is not necessarily easy to go through.

When you go through pain and keep your heart open, your capacity to receive love grows and is refined, and you are transformed. Your ability to give love, to be love, rests on your ability to receive love. When we receive love, we naturally want to give love. You can see this most directly in a child.

If you have closed off your heart, you have to do healing work to reopen your heart to love. The work is always the same. It is the work of feeling. It may be helpful to have someone guide you in the process, someone who understands the process of feeling and can guide you all the way through to the source of the feelings, the beautiful qualities or divine attributes from which the feelings emanate. Then you will be reconnected to God's love, and therein lies the healing.

Your feeling heart is a great gift. Your other great gift is your mind, and the mind can also lead you to God. What is tricky about it is that you can operate from your lower mind, which tends to separate you from God, or you can operate from your higher mind, which connects you to God. Learning to quiet your lower mind, to set it aside by choice, is helpful in opening up the higher mind. This is what you do when you meditate.

In meditation, you open up to pure awareness, which leads you to the state that I call consciousness. This has been called by other names in other traditions or by other people. Sometimes, it is called emptiness or the void. It is a state of great quietude, tranquility, and depth, in which you become aware of a stillness or centeredness that is prior to all the things that are occurring, the places and people and events. It seems beyond space and time, beyond all arising, prior to all of that. In connecting with this state, you receive a transmission of peace and presence. You might have a feeling of coming home to your true self. And that is so, for you are connecting with the qualities of God.

You can think of these as two paths to God: one is the path of love, and one is the path of consciousness. Many religious or spiritual traditions have emphasized one or the other, and some have emphasized both. They're not exclusive. The reason there are two paths is because they reflect the two "faces" or forms of God that were created in the original or first form of manifestation, which occurred in the process of devolving into the various dimensions.

Originally, there was just Source, the undifferentiated Divine, which I call Supreme Creator. In order to experience itself in form, Supreme Creator chose to manifest itself in increasingly denser levels of manifest existence, which some have called the dimensions. The first step was to manifest itself in the twelfth dimension, which is only one step removed from pure, undifferentiated Divine Being. And this first step-down of manifestation was in the form of Mother-Father God.

In this first manifestation, there was the original split into the two forms or "faces" of God, the Feminine and the Masculine. Of course, these are just names for the qualities they embody. And please remember that everyone embodies all of these qualities, whatever their gender is. Just as the God-forms in the twelfth dimension were manifested as Masculine and Feminine, so are each of you manifested in both of these forms as well, through your inner Masculine and Feminine.

The Feminine qualities of Mother God were centered on love, nurturing, compassion, feeling, wisdom, faith, intuition, devotion, and creation through form and energy. The Feminine emphasizes receptivity because she is all about receiving God's love.

The Masculine qualities of Father God are centered on awareness, consciousness, presence, choice, will, power, goal accomplishment, insight, and understanding. The Masculine emphasizes assertion and action because he is all about the action of bringing God's light.

Everyone must develop both sides of their relationship to God, their Feminine side of love and their Masculine side of consciousness. Even if you focus on only one side as your path, only on love or only on consciousness (and, indeed, some paths are quite focused on one side or the other), eventually it will bring you to the other side because, in truth, they aren't separate from each other. They are like two sides of a coin, two faces of the same Being.

The most direct path is to develop both the Masculine and the Feminine, love and consciousness. This will take you most quickly to your reunion with Source through our Mother-Father God, to your full union with undifferentiated Source, which is what all beings truly desire.

I support you in this most fully, as it is the greatest fulfillment you can experience.

In love and light, I shine my blessings upon you.
I AM Mary Magdalene

*I*n her opening statement, Mary states unequivocally that God is love and follows with the acknowledgment that love is also a path to God. The juxtaposition of these two ideas has the effect of stopping my mind. How can love (God) be the end result—and also be the path to achieve it? When she clarifies that the path of love is primarily about opening your heart to receive God's love, her statement sheds light on why I'm confused.

I tend to think of the spiritual practice of love as something that one does, something active that involves generating love and sending it out to others. But Mary isn't describing being active and doing loving things; she's talking about receiving love. I see an image of my heart opening and becoming like a bowl or a chalice, ready to receive a stream of love from God—a giant pitcher of love pouring into the eager receptacle of my heart. The path involves embodying and becoming the love that God is on the basis of having received that love.

Mary tells us that it's natural for our hearts to be open, but many of us have closed our hearts to protect ourselves from feeling pain. Sometimes this happens in childhood, sometimes when we are adults. The result is the same: we shut down our hearts and become closed off from life and love.

Closing our hearts in response to pain is the opposite of what's supposed to happen. Pain is actually meant to grow our hearts and make us more open and loving. Mary likens this to the Colorado River gradually wearing away the rock of the Grand Canyon and, in doing so, carving out its beauty.

This view of pain as something that helps us grow differs markedly from common attitudes toward pain. Some people think of pain as punishment for displeasing God. Others think of pain as just part of *the way things are*: this world is full of suffering, and we just have to cope with it as best we can. Mary sees pain as a tool for our spiritual growth in the third dimension, as something that actually supports us. If we understand it as such, we can make use of pain to grow and deepen our ability to love. If we haven't understood this and have closed off from pain, we have healing to do in order to reopen our hearts.

Mary instructs us to engage this healing by opening to feeling. When we do that, we will once again feel the pain we originally walled off so we wouldn't have to experience it. Feelings don't just disappear when we block them. It's the same as putting the feelings in a closet and closing the door: they haven't gone away; they're just out of sight. Opening to feeling is like reopening the closet door and embracing the feelings we originally stuffed inside. Mary acknowledges we may need support for this process because, unless we've become skilled in processing painful feelings, our emotions may overwhelm us.

Whether we work with a guide or on our own, the process is the same. Mary instructs us to feel all the way through to the source of the feelings, which are the beautiful qualities or divine attributes from which the feelings emanated. In doing this, she tells us, we will be reconnected to God's love, which is both the healer and the healing.

Throughout the messages, Mary emphasizes the importance of experiencing our painful feelings until we reach their source—our inner divine qualities—and in this way, our pain reconnects us with God. Because this process still isn't automatic for me, I find her repetition helpful. I've watched as, over time, my ability to open to pain and let it take me to God has become increasingly strong. Being adept in this process is especially valuable when we're under emotional duress and aren't thinking clearly. Fortunately, the more skilled we become at this, the more dependably we're able to use it.

Mary also discusses another path to God: consciously relaxing our lower mind and opening to our higher mind. This process evokes a state of peace, quiet, spaciousness, and freedom, in which our thinking mind relaxes, bringing a deep sense of unity. Many people know how to do this through meditation, but it certainly can happen in other ways. We might experience this state when we're immersed in nature, hearing beautiful music, or soaking in warm water. We might feel this connection when we first awake in the morning, when we spend time with a young child, after a good cry, or on countless other occasions. Meditation is simply a practice that allows us to strengthen our ability to access this state by choice rather than having it happen to us as a result of something else. Through meditation, we build up the "muscles" that connect us to our higher mind.

Our lower mind—the combination of our rational mind and our subconscious mind—is what I define as the ego. The lower mind serves many valuable functions that support our survival and growth, especially in the third dimension. We don't need to kill the ego, get rid of it, or become egoless to grow spiritually. It's only when the ego, or lower mind, tries to take charge that we have difficulties. The lower mind processes the world based on separation; when the mind tries to control us, we lose our connection to God. The lower mind/ego is valuable as long as it remains in service to the higher functions of our sacred heart and our sacred, or higher, mind, both of which connect us to God. That service is strengthened when the lower mind can relax at will so that we can rest in our connection to the Divine.

Mary describes what occurs when we experience the higher mind through meditation. We open up to the state that she refers to as consciousness, which is a state of great peace, depth, and stillness. As we abide in consciousness, we become aware of a centeredness that seems beyond space and time, beyond and prior to all arising. We may have a sense of the presence of God. There may be a feeling of coming home to our true selves. And we are, she tells us, for we are connecting with the qualities of God.

Mary reveals that there are two basic paths to God: the path of love and the path of consciousness. Many religious or spiritual traditions have focused primarily on one or the other, while others have included both. These two paths reflect the Feminine and Masculine aspects of creation, which began with the very first division from Undifferentiated Oneness—which Mary calls Supreme Creator—into the form of Mother-Father God. This first division into Masculine-Feminine set a pattern for all of creation in our universe, a pattern that is reflected in our outer world and also in our inner world as our inner Masculine-Feminine. And it's reflected in the two overarching spiritual paths that grew out of these two "faces," or forms, of the Divine: the path of love (Feminine based) and the path of consciousness (Masculine based).

Although Christianity has been Masculine dominated in terms of its power structure, its actual practice—with its emphasis on love, faith, and creation of God's kingdom here on Earth—provides an example of a Feminine-oriented spiritual tradition. An example of a more Masculine-oriented spiritual tradition is Buddhism, which values awareness, insight, discipline, and transcendence to a purer state. However, because all experience includes both the Masculine and the Feminine, no path is exclusively one or the other. Even paths that are predominantly Masculine or Feminine in their orientation, if fully followed, eventually lead to the other side. The wholeness at the heart of all forms of manifestation contains both polarities.

Mary suggests that the most direct path of spiritual growth integrates both aspects: Masculine and Feminine, consciousness and love. Although she speaks as an advocate for the Feminine path of God, which has been suppressed and overshadowed for so long, she never speaks in opposition to the Masculine path. Rather, she advocates for balance and union of the Feminine with the Masculine. I believe she and Yeshua embodied this balance and union in their relationship. Now I hear her calling all of us to the same balance and union. For most of us, that requires strengthening the Feminine.

You might call Mary a modern-day spiritual coach or trainer who is helping us all to strengthen our Feminine side so that we may attain balance and union with the Masculine. She views our under-developed Feminine strength and power as what is holding us at our current level of spiritual evolution. Through her instructions about engaging both sides of our being, Mary offers us the keys to unlock that strength and power, and thereby open the floodgates to our next level of spiritual development.

PART IV

A New Way
of Relating to Life

ELEVEN

Ending Projection

My dear beloved ~

Today, I come to you to talk about a particular pattern that you and so many people at this time have learned, one that is doing great harm to you. This pattern involves directing your pain outward toward others.

Very many people have learned to protect themselves from pain by immediately, as soon as they become aware of being in pain, finding someone or something outside themselves to blame for that pain. This relates to emotional pain primarily but can also apply to physical pain. As soon as something happens that you don't like, that makes you uncomfortable, or that you fear, you look for something or someone outside yourself to focus on, to say that they caused this. And then you spend a great deal of time and energy being upset with them, being angry at them, and talking about them, either to others or inside your head. You build up a whole case against them, proving that they were wrong, that what they did was wrong, and that you are the injured or "wronged" party. Often, you try to get others to agree with your point of view.

All the while, what you are really doing is distracting yourself from your actual pain by focusing on those outside yourself. This is an unfortunate choice because pain serves a purpose, and you are denying yourself the benefit of that purpose by distracting yourself from your pain. Pain is a warning signal; it is your being communicating to you that something is not serving you, that something needs changing. When you distract yourself from your pain by focusing on others, you are spending your energy thinking about them instead of being with your pain. So your energy is not used to help you change, and because of this, you stay stuck. You are telling yourself it's not about you, that it's the others who need to change because they were the ones who were wrong. So you do nothing but complain and grow bitter and wait for them to change.

You will change by doing this because you will poison yourself with your own anger, bitterness, and resentment. This will harm you. You will change by shutting down your heart, and this will affect your life negatively, reducing your happiness and joy, perhaps interfering with your relationships because of walls and barriers you erect, perhaps hurting you physically and affecting your health, and also poisoning your mind with thoughts that others are trying to hurt you.

This is not the kind of change that pain is intended for. The kind of change that pain is meant for is your growth and opening in light and love. Pain is a gift that is given to support you. For this to happen, you must open yourself to the pain rather than running from it, avoiding it, and distracting yourself by blaming others and focusing on them. *Do not project your pain onto others.* Yes, others may have done things that you didn't like or that affected you in certain ways, but your pain is your own. Do not project it onto others. Understand the difference between their actions and your pain. Do not create more pain by projecting your pain outward onto others.

Instead, open yourself to the pain. It will not destroy you. Feel it, experience it, and ask God to help you with it. Ask God to take it. Ask God to guide you to the highest and best responses that will support you to change and grow in your opening to light and love, in your becoming light and love. Ask God to direct you to what is in the best interest and for the highest good of all involved. Then you are not setting yourself up as the opponent of all others. You are joining with God and all others in this great ocean of unity that we are all swimming in.

Beloved, this is the highest path, and it is a path of joy, even when there is pain. Pain is a part of your third-dimensional existence, and it is such because it helps you to grow. As you grow and evolve into higher dimensions, you won't require pain for this kind of growth. But in this dimension, it is given as a form of help. So make use of it.

The beauty is that when you respond to pain in this way, your heart is gladdened, uplifted, enlightened. You become joyful. So your rewards are immediate and you yourself will enjoy the difference right away. In your terms, you might call this instant karma. You instantly get the results of your choice.

You will feel worse and worse and be more and more unhappy, the more you project your pain outward onto others. You will feel more and more light and love, the more you experience and open to your pain, give it to God, and let God direct you. This is not the same as denying your pain. You are not saying that you have no pain or that nothing happened. You are fully feeling and being with it. But don't stop there. That is the first step, and then you take the next steps. You give your pain to God, and you ask God to direct you to whatever is for the highest good of all involved.

This will set you free. This will bring you peace and joy. This will unite you with the Beloved of your heart, God, as well as with yourself and all others. This is the gift of pain.

I love you, and I offer you this insight.
I AM Mary Magdalene

*I*n this message, Mary addresses projection, a particular strategy many people use to avoid feeling pain. This tactic is usually engaged as soon as we find ourselves in pain: immediately, we project the pain outward onto others. I have an image of someone literally throwing pain away from their body, like a hot potato, onto some external "other." Most often, we do this before we even notice that we're in pain. Instead of experiencing the feeling, we focus our attention on how others have harmed us and why they're wrong. This outward focus effectively masks, or distracts, us from feeling our pain. We're now caught up in our minds and consumed with judgments about others and their wrongness.

Releasing and going beyond judgment is part of the process of growing into the fourth dimension. Yet, I've heard many people say that despite how much they desire to let go of this tendency, they still find themselves persistently judging others. Mary gives us an essential clue as to why giving up judgment is so difficult: If we want to change a pattern, we need to go to the root to understand the function of the pattern. And the root of judging others and making them wrong is that it allows us to avoid feeling our pain. We believe the pain will hurt us—maybe even overwhelm and obliterate us— so our avoidance acts as a kind of self-preservation.

However, Mary assures us that feeling our pain isn't going to destroy or damage us; it's actually going to help us. Once again, she reminds us that, in the third dimension, pain is given to help us. To receive that help, however, we need to open to the pain, let it in, and embrace it. We need to let it take us to God. That's its real function. Then we can give our pain to God, ask God to take it, and ask God to direct our actions.

Mary says that pain is a warning signal that something is going on with us that needs to change. Here again, as in chapter two, I liken it to the warning light on the dashboard of a car. If it goes on and you ignore it, you're not going to benefit from that warning. If you continue to dismiss the warning, change will still happen, but it probably won't be a change you'll enjoy.

Similarly, if we distract ourselves from our pain by directing our energy outward toward others and what's wrong with them, we'll experience change, but it probably won't be a change that supports our well-being. We may grow resentful or hardened, we may shut down, or we may suffer physically. Mary refers to this as poisoning ourselves with our own anger and bitterness.

The good news is, we have a choice: We can do something else, something that will actually support our growth and well-being and help us to change. We can open to feeling our pain rather than deflecting it onto others. We can let it in and let it take us to Source. This Feminine path of opening and receiving is available to both men and women.

Because my habitual pattern is to close off from pain, it's difficult for me to open to it. When I do allow myself to open to pain, I literally feel my heart being stretched and expanded beyond my comfort zone.

I don't think this kind of resistance is the natural condition of human beings. Young children don't seem to resist pain; in fact, they immediately express their pain without holding back or deflecting it elsewhere. Unfortunately, most of us have been taught to separate from our pain, to redirect it onto others, or to somehow deny or suppress it. We may have received an overt instruction, as in, "There, there, don't cry," or we may simply have copied what was modeled to us by others who were avoiding their pain. Either way, now we need to relearn how to embrace pain.

After opening to our pain, the next step is to ask God for help and guidance on what we should do. Asking for help in this way is a Feminine response. The archetypical Feminine knows how to ask for help. In my case, asking God for help often doesn't occur to me. Having been raised in our modern Masculine-based culture, I'm oriented toward handling life on my own. Because of this, I appreciate Mary's reminder that we can always seek help and that asking is a great path of joy. She directs us to ask God to guide us to the highest good for all.

I'm particularly struck by her comment that including the best interests of everyone in the outcome is doing something counter to our usual activity of setting ourselves up as the opponent of others. Instead, as Mary says, we're "joining with God and all others in this great ocean of unity that we are all swimming in."

What happens when we respond to pain by embracing it and letting God guide us? In Mary's words, "your heart is gladdened, uplifted, enlightened. You become joyful."

I've come to recognize a predictable process that ensues when I stop avoiding pain. First, I come to a place of feeling peaceful and reconnected with Spirit. Next, my painful feelings fade or dissolve. During this time, I may receive a new understanding or insight. As I integrate this new perspective, I sense that parts of myself become connected in a new, more functional way that's more aligned to God. Then, before I know it, my energy is flowing and I'm available to engage life, feeling stronger, more open, and happier.

Perhaps as I acquire more mastery in responding to pain, these steps will happen faster, with more ease and grace, and I will immediately experience my heart being gladdened, uplifted, and enlightened. I certainly hope so! Yet, even now, this process transpires in a relatively short time. What is more, I've come to feel excited when I have an opportunity to embrace pain because I trust where it will lead me. That doesn't mean I invite pain or look to increase it in my life. I simply am able to consciously receive it as a gift when it does show up.

Mary makes a final, important point about the difference between denying pain and experiencing light and love as a result of opening to pain. Through denial, you're saying that you have no pain, that nothing happened. Denying pain is comparable to covering over the warning lights on your dashboard with duct tape or decorative stickers. By contrast, when you open to pain, you fully feel and are with your pain, and this connects you to God. Then, in Mary's words, "you give your pain to God, and you ask God to direct you to whatever is for the highest good of all involved."

If we do this, Mary tells us what will happen: It will set us free. It will bring us peace and joy. It will unite us with the Beloved of our hearts, God, as well as with ourselves and all others. This is the gift of pain.

And to that I say, "So be it!"

TWELVE

The Embrace of All

Greetings again, beloved ~

You are correct that I have more to say. I am aware that I have been speaking to you a great deal about pain and about how to respond to pain and receive its gifts. I am guessing that you are wondering why it is necessary to focus so much on pain and why I'm not speaking more about joy and God and beautiful things that inspire you and open your heart.

This is an important question and one that I'm happy to address. It is somewhat complex for me to explain, so my answer will have several parts to it.

First of all, many of you have the idea that pain is the opposite of pleasure. Many of you like pleasure and don't like pain. You tend to see one as good (pleasure) and one as bad (pain). You tend to want to have as much pleasure as possible and as little pain as possible. So you are driven to seek pleasure and avoid pain.

This is one result of relating to the world in duality. In actuality, you cannot have pleasure without pain. They are simply relative qualities that only have meaning in relationship to each other. You only consider something pleasurable because it is different from your usual state. The same is true of pain. If you only had pleasure and no pain, yet were still thinking within a dualistic framework, you would simply create increments of pain within what you used to call pleasure. That is the nature of the mind. It is always comparing one thing to another.

So the idea of getting away from pain and only having pleasure is an illusion and a trap. If you are thinking that way, you are committing yourself to an endless path of seeking and avoidance that will never be fruitful. Not only will it not be fruitful, it will take you away from another path that could be very fruitful.

Pain is an inherent part of third-dimensional reality. Therefore, feeling pain is also an inherent part of third-dimensional reality. Yet, many of you have been trained to think that it's possible to avoid pain by denying that you have any pain or by seeking to eliminate it and only have pleasure. Oddly, you have not noticed that both of these strategies are not only ineffective, but they actually bring about more pain. Such is the strength of the mind that it can continue to believe certain things even in the face of evidence to the contrary.

Because this pattern of denying and avoiding pain is so endemic to your society, so pervasive in people's thinking in this day and age, I am choosing to emphasize this arena in my talks to try to counteract this train of thinking and to show you a different possibility. Why, you might ask, are other spiritual teachers not focusing on pain? Why are you not talking about the kinds of things they're talking about, such as rising above pain into higher things?

It is true that I am focusing a great deal on responding to pain, as well as on relating to the physical reality, valuing feelings and emotions, and honoring sexuality as sacred. It is also true that these are topics that many spiritual teachers are not addressing, though certainly some are. And there is a particular reason why this is so. It has to do with the embrace, over a great deal of time, of the Sacred Feminine.

As I have explained before, originally there was only the Supreme

Creator, the one undifferentiated Source of All That Is. The first creation of form, the initial step-down from Supreme Creator, was the manifestation into Mother-Father God. Mother God brought forth the Sacred Feminine qualities, and Father God brought forth the Sacred Masculine qualities.

All individuals have the Sacred Feminine and the Sacred Masculine within themselves. Yet, for many thousands of years, the path of the Sacred Masculine has dominated and the path of the Sacred Feminine has become suppressed. This is shifting now, yet this is not an easy shift—for men or women—because you are battling the indoctrination of several thousands of years.

I support the Sacred Feminine in coming into balance once again with the Sacred Masculine. Yeshua and I understood the balance of the Sacred Feminine and Masculine, and we lived this together. We embodied these two paths within ourselves, as well as living the unity of the Sacred Feminine and Masculine with each other. Yet, this aspect of our lives was not recognized or received by the masses. It was not time for this, and we both understood that. Now people are ready to hear and receive this other aspect of our divinity, the Divine Feminine.

And so I am speaking to you of other areas of life than you typically associate with spirituality because most of you associate spirituality with the Divine Masculine approach. In truth, you must ultimately master and embody both. Yet, most people have a deficit relative to understanding and embracing the Divine Feminine because of your imbalanced history of excluding that aspect and path. So now I am emphasizing that to bring about balance.

The Feminine is the path of embracing all aspects of life to take you to Source. Most of you find it easy to embrace pleasure (though not always, as that, too, can feel threatening, especially if it's more pleasure than you're used to). The part that is difficult for most of you is embracing pain. So I am focusing on that to help you to change your thinking and your approach in this area because it is such a barrier to your spiritual growth if you don't understand how to do this.

The Masculine is the path of transcendence of all to take you to Source. This is a difficult path for most people, too, as it requires discipline of body and mind. Yet, most who are dedicated to the spiritual path have come to accept this to some extent or other.

The truth is that both are required. And one inevitably leads to the other. Transcendence inevitably leads to embrace of all, just as embrace of all ultimately leads to transcendence. The nature of one is to be in unity with the other. And if either is neglected or underdeveloped, it thwarts the other. So I am choosing to focus on the key areas where I see the energy of people's evolution being blocked, like a kink in a hose that the water isn't able to pass through.

One of the biggest arenas in which people are blocked in their embrace of life is in the area of responding to pain. That is why I am addressing this so directly and repeatedly—to help people come into right relationship in this area so that they are not stopped from the full embrace of life that leads to unity with all. I am a dedicated advocate of unity with all, as I have known this path as a powerful and direct channel for union with God. And union with God is my love and my passion.

I am holding you in the light of our Mother-Father God
and showering you with blessings.
I AM Mary Magdalene

*I*n this communication, Mary explains why she focuses so much on how to respond to pain and why her guidance seems different from that of other spiritual teachers. Many of us have the idea that it's possible to attain a state of pleasure and be free of pain. Because many believe this is achievable, they spend their lives pursuing pleasure and doing their best to avoid pain.

However, Mary points out that the idea of being able to live in the third dimension in a state of pleasure that's free from pain is an illusion. Because the third dimension is a realm of duality, qualities such as pleasure exist only in relation to their opposites, in this case pain. Even if we were able to eliminate pain, we would re-create it out of what was formerly pleasurable for us because that's the nature of our dualistic perception.

My partner and I used to have a weekly business selling plants and produce at a farmers market. The first time we brought in a thousand dollars in one day, we were ecstatic and felt free of financial worries, at least for the moment. Over time, as we achieved that level of profit and more on a regular basis, we no longer felt thrilled by receiving that amount of money. Taking in a thousand dollars had become just part of routine business, and now it took much more for us to get relief from our financial concerns.

Our inability to eliminate pain and struggle in our lives, combined with our belief that it is possible to do so, forms a fertile breeding ground for addictions, which are simply behavior patterns for denying, avoiding, and suppressing pain. Of course, addictions aren't limited to alcohol or drugs. They include any pattern of behavior that's compulsively employed to avoid pain. These behaviors can be socially accepted and even respected, such as workaholism, achievement of the "good life" of material comfort, relationship addiction, spiritual addiction, and so forth. In other words, any repetitive behavior or habit that's being used to avoid pain can be a form of addiction.

The danger in attempting to eliminate pain is twofold. First, it doesn't work: in general, the things we do to avoid pain end up generating more pain. For example, in drug addiction, the drug usage starts to generate its own problems, such as erratic or dangerous behavior, disruption of relationships and families, health problems, and so on. The behaviors that were originally employed to escape pain have now become a source of pain themselves.

Therefore, the first problem with avoiding pain is that it leads to more pain. The second problem is that addictions divert us from something valuable—the opportunity to make use of pain to lead us to God. This might be called "the gift of pain." Mary needs to keep repeating her message about pain because of the degree to which most of us are engaged in avoiding it. Our programming to avoid pain is a primary obstacle to our growth, and she is dedicated to helping us through and beyond this barrier.

Later in this message, Mary responds to our unspoken question about why other teachers don't address the issue of our response to pain in the same way she does here. In fact, many spiritual teachers and teachings have addressed pain and how to respond to it. For the most part, however, their orientation and recommendations have been significantly different from Mary's.

This is because, until quite recently, most spiritual teachings have represented the Divine Masculine qualities that Mary describes as being based on transcendence. For example, in some schools of Buddhism and Hinduism, people engage in practices such as meditation, mindfulness, and right living in order to overcome suffering. This approach is based on transcending, or going beyond, suffering, so that one is liberated from bondage to suffering. The suffering is replaced by spiritual practices, which eventually lead to the preferred state of liberation or enlightenment.

I picture this path as replacing something less desirable with certain behaviors that lead to something more desirable. This kind of going-away-from the undesirable and toward a desired destination is an archetypically Masculine activity: There's a goal and actions are engaged to lead one to the goal. Practitioners are usually guided by intention, awareness, and discernment, and they utilize discipline of the body and mind to attain the desired results.

In the new-age spiritual movement, this same kind of Masculine orientation can be seen in the law-of-attraction work and New Thought spirituality. Followers of these paths believe their thoughts create their reality. Their practice involves staying aware of their thoughts and beliefs, discerning the results of different kinds of thinking, and making a choice about the kinds of thoughts they engage in so as to achieve the kind of reality they would like. The discipline in this path is one of controlling one's thoughts and their expression.

Mary doesn't say that these paths are wrong or need to be let go of, and she acknowledges that the Divine Masculine approach is valid and effective. What she is saying, though, is that this approach is partial; it's only half of the picture. The other half is the Divine Feminine approach of embracing all of life as the Divine. In particular, it involves embracing the Feminine parts of ourselves—our bodies, emotions, and sexuality—as these are the parts that have been particularly excluded from our history of Masculine-dominated spirituality.

I visualize the Masculine-oriented approach as going toward a goal, like an arrow shooting toward the mark. I see the Feminine-oriented approach as an inward opening and softening and expansion that allows all to come in, like a mother embracing all her children in her arms of love. In the path of the Divine Feminine, the embraced "children" are all forms of arising phenomena, including pain.

The image of a mother's embrace includes another aspect of the Feminine path: it's about love and opening our hearts to love. While most religions include love as one of their principles, they simply recommend that people live as love but don't tell us how to do this.

I suggest that this recommendation hasn't been sufficient for most of us. If it were, we would already be living our lives as love. We do live as love, some of the time and to some extent, but most spiritually oriented people will acknowledge that they're not living the principle of love as fully as they would like. Mary's practical instruction in the Feminine aspects of our lives fills in this gap by giving us concrete steps for incarnating love.

Mary offers her relationship with Yeshua as the perfect model of balance between the Feminine and the Masculine:

> Yeshua and I understood the balance of the Sacred Feminine and Masculine, and we lived this together. We embodied these two paths within ourselves, as well as living the unity of the Sacred Feminine and Masculine with each other. Yet, this aspect of our lives was not recognized or received by the masses. It was not time for this, and we both understood that. Now people are ready to hear and receive this other aspect of our divinity, the Divine Feminine.

Mary clarifies that the path of the Divine Masculine ultimately leads to the Divine Feminine and vice versa. I have met Buddhist practitioners who emanate tremendous love, and I've heard teachings from Mother Theresa or Christian mystics whose path is about love and surrender, yet who have obvious clarity and consciousness in their communications. If the Masculine and Feminine eventually converge, you may wonder why we need to focus on the Divine Feminine. Why isn't it sufficient to stay with the current teachings, which—even if they're focused on Masculine-oriented practices—will eventually lead us to the Divine Feminine?

I can address this from my personal experience. When I first began my spiritual search as a teenager and young adult, I tried a variety of spiritual practices I believed could lead me to union with

God. I wasn't drawn to either Christianity or Judaism because I didn't feel a connection with their teachings or practices. So I tried hatha yoga, mantra meditation, the breathing meditations of Zen Buddhism, and all the practices Ram Dass suggested in his groundbreaking book, *Be Here Now*. All these practices involved the discipline of stilling the mind to achieve more elevated states, and I was a miserable failure at all of them. I resisted all discipline, my mind never stopped spinning and generating endless thoughts, and I actually got migraine headaches every time I engaged in Zen meditation. While I had the intuition that these were authentic paths to something I desired, I didn't seem to have it in me to do what it took to get there.

Then, in my early twenties, I was introduced to a spiritual teacher who included two different approaches to spiritual growth—a path of devotion and a path of insight—because he observed that different types of people respond to different avenues of spiritual engagement. As it turned out, most of the women followers of this teaching engaged in the path of devotion, and most of the men followers engaged in the path of insight. Immediately, I felt drawn to the practice of devotion and was relieved and excited to discover I seemed to have an affinity for this path. I wasn't a failure at spirituality; I just needed to find a path that engaged my natural tendencies and strengths.

After having a significant spiritual opening, I switched to the path of insight, and for awhile I found value in those practices. Eventually I returned to the path of devotion, and since then I have generally found the devotional orientation to be more suited to my nature. I consider devotion-based spirituality to be a Feminine-oriented path, exemplified by worship of gurus, exalted beings, or deities with specific forms and personalities. I now see the path of insight, on the other hand, as a more Masculine-oriented path, with the primary focus on awareness practices, such as asking oneself the question, who am I? or working with the koans of Zen Buddhism.

I've encountered many people who've told me that they just can't meditate. When people say this, they're generally talking about the Masculine-oriented approach to meditation, which involves sitting still in a cross-legged pose for an extended period of time and using a particular technique to quiet the mind. When I offer these people a more Feminine approach that includes finding a comfortable position, using music or drumming, engaging in guided-imagery that includes all the senses, supporting the person in relating to other beings and realms, and engaging their creative powers, they almost always have profound spiritual experiences that they find very satisfying.

Because we're all made up of both Feminine and Masculine qualities and aspects, it's most helpful to have practices that address and include *both* of these parts of ourselves. Many people, like me, have a primary affinity toward one approach or the other. But at certain times, or in certain circumstances, we'll be helped by the other approach. This is why having access to both is extremely beneficial; otherwise, we're deprived of valuable support that includes all the parts of ourselves.

As we move more and more into unity consciousness, embracing the Feminine path and the Feminine aspects of ourselves along with the Masculine becomes increasingly important. Mary offers her insightful guidance to help break up the logjam in the river of our spiritual development that has resulted from the exclusion of the Feminine. I greatly appreciate her courage and dedication to freeing us from these limits.

THIRTEEN

Birthing Your Divine Self

Beloved one ~

Greetings again. I come to you in love, to share the light and wonder of our Creator God.

On this day, I ask you to open your heart. I ask you to open your mind. I ask you to open to life. I ask you to open to love, which is always God's love. And I ask you to open to light, which is always God's light. It is that simple. Your job is to open, and God will do the rest.

Let your mind be focused on love and light. Let your heart be full of love and light. Let your actions be directed by love and light. It is that simple.

When you have lost your connections with love and light, simply notice it. Notice that your mind is full of thoughts that occlude love and light, like clouds blocking the sun. Notice that your heart has become closed and your body has become tight. If you open your heart through feeling, and open your body through relaxing, and if you clear your mind through breathing, you will notice that what's at the root of this occlusion is some form of pain, usually emotional pain. You are hurt or scared or sad. If you remain open in your heart and body and mind, you will be able to feel the pain. And in that openness, you can ask God to take the pain and to direct you.

This is what is called surrender. Surrender is not about losing or being defeated. It's an act of reconnecting with God. You are surrendering once again to the beauty of light and love. You are surrendering your shutting off, tightening down, closing off from God. Why did you shut down, close off, tighten away from God? Because you were in pain, and you were afraid of the pain. This is the critical point, the crucial moment of choice. You can choose to contract away from your pain or to open to it.

You see, you don't shut off just from pain. You shut off from pain, yes, but you also shut off from life and God. So you have a choice. You can shut off from pain and life and God, or you can open to pain and life and God. It's that simple. And if you choose to open to pain and life and God, you will likely be surprised. It won't be what you probably expect. You think that opening to pain will increase the pain, will overwhelm you, might even be so strong that you won't survive. Yet, it's just the opposite. Opening to pain actually allows the pain to do its job. It's only when you close off from pain, tighten down upon it, that the pain becomes fixed, stuck—and this actually creates more pain. The tightening becomes fuel that adds to the pain. When you open to pain, it becomes diffuse, more watery. It's like the pain is "unclothed," and you experience it more in its source form. Then pain becomes a medium of movement, an avenue or stream of feeling that carries you to God.

This is the River of Life, and it always carries you to God. Let go of swimming upstream, against the current. Go with the River of Life and let it carry you to God.

This was the great breakthrough of the natural childbirth movement. It became understood that women had a choice in childbirth to relax and open to the experience, even in the midst of tremendous intensity and pain, and this transformed the event. Women didn't need anesthetic to remove the pain. They were able to flow with the intensity through relaxation and breathing. They allowed the birth to happen and supported it, rather than resisting it. And this not only allowed them to go through the event, but it also allowed the birth to happen naturally and organically.

When you are in pain, you are in the process of giving birth to a new part of yourself. You can cooperate with the event and support it, just like a natural childbirth. By learning to open to your feelings, relax the body, and breathe to clear the mind, you will support this birth, this new part of yourself. And in so doing, you can allow yourself to surrender to God. Then what will be born is a new part of your God-self. What a glorious event and cause for celebration.

I am here to midwife you in the birthing of your God-self. You are a wondrous being of light and love. Light and love are always available to you. Your pain simply informs you of when you have shut down upon it. Use that knowledge to support you in reopening to light and love.

I AM Mary Magdalene, and I love you most deeply.

The simplicity of this message touches me deeply. Mary is asking us to open our hearts, minds, and bodies to God's love and light. She tells us that it is that simple: our job is to open, and God will do the rest. Of course, something simple isn't necessarily easy. But simplicity is a wonderful start: When something is simple, we have clarity about our choices.

What does opening to God look like? Mary tells us it's about focusing our minds on light and love, filling our hearts with light and love, and letting our actions be directed by light and love. Light and love don't just happen to us, like lucky charms falling out of the sky. We must choose, moment by moment, to connect with light and love. There are many ways to make this connection. We can do it by engaging in meditation or other spiritual practices. We can do it through our words, by expressing gratitude, compassion, and joy rather than criticism, judgment, and blame. We can do it through choosing to receive communications from people who connect us to light and love, rather than from those who focus on fear and lack. We can do it through actions that bring light and love to us and others. Most of all, we can do it as an ongoing practice, through staying heart-connected to light and love in our feeling.

But what if we don't feel light and love? This is an essential question because this practice isn't about assuming a Pollyanna-like disposition and acting in ways that aren't authentic. Mary isn't advocating suppression. She says when we've lost our connection to light and love, the first step is to simply notice it. Notice if the mind is full of thoughts, if the heart is closed, or if the body is tight. She then explains how to shift the mind/body state. We can engage our feelings to open the heart. We can consciously relax to open the body. And we can breathe deeply and fully to clear the mind.

When we do this, Mary tells us that we'll notice what's at the root of our disconnection from light and love. Our thought-filled mind, closed heart, and tight body were all blocking something, like clouds occluding the sun. When we open through feeling, relaxing, and breathing, we connect with the underlying layer. There, we will usually find some kind of emotional pain: we're either hurt or scared or sad.

The next step is critical. Once we notice and feel our pain, we can ask God to take it and direct us from there. This is what Mary calls surrender, which she says isn't about losing or being defeated. It's about reconnecting with God. We give up our resistance to God. We give up our shutting off, tightening down, and closing away from God. We let go of our contraction away from pain and choose instead to open to it. And through that, we open to life and God.

Mary emphasizes two things in this process. One is that the choice to shut off from pain doesn't just block pain; it also shuts us off from life and God. Her other point is that if we choose to open to pain, and thus also to life and God, it's likely the outcome won't be what we expect. Most of us assume, at some level, that opening to pain will increase our experience of it, perhaps even to the point of burying us in pain. In fact, Mary reassures us that the reverse is true. Resisting pain holds it in place, while opening to pain allows it to move, complete its work, resolve itself, and dissolve. Some people have described the word *emotion* as *e-motion*, or energy-in-motion. Allowing our emotions, or feelings, to move, rather than holding them back and keeping them stuck, permits them to move through their natural cycle: we experience and possibly express the emotion and then let it carry us to the source of the feeling, which is ultimately the Divine.

Mary calls this natural movement the River of Life. She tells us to "let go of swimming upstream, against the current. Go with the River of Life and let it carry you to God." Experiencing our pain is a significant part of flowing with the River of Life, and trying to stave it off is like swimming against the current. Mary calls out to us, "Let go—trust the current." She compares this to natural childbirth, where women learn to open to the powerful experience of labor through relaxing, breathing, and feeling so that they don't need anesthetics to handle the pain of contractions. Instead, they can flow with the contractions, cooperate with the body, and experience a natural childbirth. Similarly, she says that when we're in pain, we're giving birth to a new part of ourselves. I love this image! She guides us to support this birth by opening to it—through feeling, relaxing, breathing, giving our pain to God, and asking God to guide us. What is birthed then is a greater part of our God-self.

Mary calls herself a midwife for the birth of our God-self. And like all good midwives, she encourages us to move through our fear and despair—lighting the way ahead of us, coaching us in how to traverse our passage, and reassuring us that it's all worthwhile. Mary's final words in this message sing forth with her confidence in this process:

> You are a wondrous being of light and love. Light and love are always available to you. Your pain simply informs you of when you have shut down upon it. Use that knowledge to support you in reopening to light and love.

FOURTEEN

Lifting the Veil around Abundance and Death

Hello, beloved ~

Today, I want to speak about an aspect of the Sacred Feminine that is very central to the challenges you face in your world today and the consciousness that will allow you to grow beyond these challenges. What I want to talk to you about is the consciousness of inclusion.

Most people at this time have been trained to think of the world as a physical reality that has finite resources. You've been trained to think that there is only a certain amount of resources available to you and that often there aren't enough resources to satisfy the needs and wants of everyone. Because of this perceived limitation of resources, you've also been trained to think that everyone can't have enough, and certainly can't have everything that they want, because there isn't enough to go around.

You've also been trained to think that people are inherently greedy and selfish. This is based on the idea that people are not that far removed from animals, and that people's animal nature is to be competitive, to fight for resources for themselves, and to not care about others or their effect on others. You might call this idea "the dog-eat-dog world."

These ideas tend to generate a lot of fear in people—fear that there won't be enough for them and their loved ones, fear that they can't trust others because everyone is just out for their own survival, and fear that if they help others survive, there will be less for them.

These ideas have actually been promoted by those who want to control you. Once people are in a state of fear, they become open to the idea that they need authority figures—individuals with power to "keep the peace" and keep them safe from others who are competing with them for the limited resources. There has been an agenda by some to maintain this state of fear—through these ideas of limited resources and danger from those around you who want to harm you—for their own profit and survival. Then you will think you need an individual or group to take control in order to keep you safe. Once you, and people in general, are convinced of this, it's a relatively easy next step to get people to agree to be controlled, to give their power to the authorities, who tell people they will keep them safe.

You should always be cautious of anyone who supports ideas based on fear. Today, there are many people who would have you believe that you're in danger and should act out of fear. In truth, the greatest danger you face is to believe it, to accept this logic, and to give these individuals your power. You are all very powerful creators. When you accept the idea that you're in danger and there is something to be afraid of, that is what you manifest. If your political leaders convince you that there is danger from another country and you empower them to send people to war, you have actually created danger for many people.

You also have the power to create peace, to create a loving and compassionate and caring world. Do you believe this? The degree to which you believe it is what will determine how much it actually manifests. Yet, it is very hard to accept this if you are still believing the base assumptions that you live in a world of lack and deficiency, populated by humans who are a threat to each other and motivated by competition. These assumptions are the root cause of a great deal of the difficulties you face in your world today.

There is an antidote to these assumptions, a whole other way of relating to the world, and it has everything to do with the Sacred Feminine. This is the missing piece that is so essential for shifting humans into a new way of being and relating. Again, I must remind you that I am not talking about gender, about women versus men. I'm talking about the qualities of the Sacred Feminine, which we all have. These are qualities of the Divine that we're all longing for because they're inherent to our very nature.

The Sacred Feminine assumes abundance, the infinite abundance of creative potential and ultimately the infinite abundance of the Divine itself. You might think of a baby who assumes the infinite abundance of its mother's milk. The child doesn't think, "There may not be enough milk for later, so I should save some and not drink it all now." No, the infant is simply aware of its hunger and assumes that there will always be enough, that the mother source will always be available.

You might ask, "What happens if there actually isn't enough milk? Will the baby continue to assume abundance?" This is when the Sacred Masculine quality comes into play, making use of creative intelligence to find other sources of food. And it is valuable to have both, to have the grounding of abundance and, within that context, the creative fuel of manifestation of the new. This is the greatest gift to give a child: the knowledge and access to both. Let them know that they live in a world of abundance, including abundant love and abundant creativity. And let them know that they have the power to create through their will and intention and mind, the power to manifest what they want.

These two ideas of abundance and the power of manifestation may be difficult for you to accept, perhaps even difficult for you to imagine, if you have been thoroughly steeped in the ideas that you live in a world of lack, deficiency, and deprivation, and that you are powerless to take care of yourselves and must depend on others who are stronger for your safety and care. Yet, I tell you that this is actually the truth of you and your world. You live in an amazing world of endless abundance, and you are incredibly powerful creators.

And now we come to the real question that so many of you have, the question that's at the root of so much of your doubt. And that question is, What about death? If we live in an abundant realm and we're so powerful, why do we die? This is such an important question because it is the root of much of why you live and act the way you do.

Suppose there was no death. How would that change the way you live and relate to life, to yourself, to others? If there was no death, you probably wouldn't feel lack. Is that not so? Most of your feeling of lack and fear that there won't be enough is based on survival, a fear of death, and your awareness, always in the back of your consciousness, of your mortality. You fear that death is the end, and you don't want to "lose" your life.

You have this fear because you have a veil over your remembering. This is part of the process you agreed to in choosing to manifest in third-dimensional reality. In this reality, there is a veil over your remembering of all the lifetimes you have lived and of all the other realms you have been in between your lifetimes. There is a veil over your remembering of your greater self, which is so much larger than the part of you that you're aware of in this third-dimensional reality. And there is a veil over your absolute connection to, your absolute inherence in, God. If you could remember all that and know it as your present-time and never-changing reality, you wouldn't have the idea of death that so many of you have. You would see death as a change of clothes, like a snake shedding its skin. When you die, you've outgrown your physical circumstances and you're ready to move on to something that's going to serve your next phase of your soul's journey. You might think of it as being something like getting a new car.

And, yes, you will be reunited with your loved ones when you die. You'll even be reunited with your loved ones who are still alive in this world because when you die, the veil of forgetfulness that masks your ability to connect between the dimensions and worlds is lifted, and you will remember how to connect with those in different worlds or realities or dimensions. Some of you in this world are already remembering this, already awakening to your ability to connect with others through the dimensions or different realities. Those who have opened to their psychic abilities are able to do this.

Even if you're not yet open to your psychic abilities, you still have a sense of longing for union. Many of you try to fulfill this in your intimate relationships, seeking the fulfillment of that longing from your partner. Yet, you're often disappointed because you're looking in the wrong place. The union you're truly seeking is union with your whole self, your greater self, and even your greatest Self, which is God. This is the only union that will fulfill you. When you know that union, you will know that all is God, and you will enjoy that union through all your relationships and all your interactions. Every moment and circumstance will be a celebration of your union with God.

And this is why you are always in a circumstance of abundance, because you are always united with the abundance of God, and God is infinite and limitless. And it's also why you are infinitely creative and capable of manifesting whatever you choose, because you are a cocreator, nonseparate from the Supreme Creator.

I am aware that I have detoured from my original topic of the consciousness of inclusiveness. I chose to do this to illuminate the context in which this shift can occur. And because I have said a great deal and given you much to consider, I will end here for now and continue this explanation at another time.

I love you and embrace you in your striving to grow.
I AM Mary Magdalene

*I*n this message, Mary delves into some of our core convictions and illuminates the truth behind those ideas. First, she addresses our assumption of deficiency: our belief that we live in a world where there isn't enough for everyone. For many of us, this lack of "enough-ness" permeates our thinking, starting with our relationship to the basic resources needed for survival. At a core level, we're anxious that there isn't enough food, water, shelter, clothing, healthcare, and so on, to sustain us. This sense of lack expands outward, manifesting as concern over not enough money, time, energy, knowledge, support, love, or care. Eventually, we feel this deficit in our relationship with ourselves, becoming convinced we aren't enough: we're not good enough, smart enough, rich enough, successful enough, talented enough, attractive enough, healthy enough, or whatever.

Mary challenges this idea that there isn't enough and we're not enough. We believe in scarcity, she asserts, because we've been trained to think our resources are limited and aren't sufficient to satisfy everyone's needs. This is an idea that's been promoted; it's not just "the way things are."

Even though I'm familiar with the new-age concept of the abundance of the universe and deeply want to believe it, Mary's spotlight on the assumption of deficiency hits a bull's eye with me. I can feel a sense of lack embedded in my subconscious; the idea of abundance feels like a lightweight facade, covering this powerful and deeply entrenched belief in lack. However, like all subconscious beliefs, its power begins to dissolve by the simple act of bringing it into the light of conscious awareness.

A second belief that goes hand-in-hand with the assumption of deficiency is the idea that humans are fundamentally selfish and greedy—that, basically, we're just animals fighting for our own survival, without a care for others. Mary refers to this as what we call "the dog-eat-dog world." I feel a strong urge at this point to say, "Hey, I don't think that's an accurate representation of animals. I've seen countless examples of animals caring for others." I think Mary would agree with this. Moreover, she would say it's also not an accurate representation of humans. Humans are capable of being deeply caring, yet many of us have been trained to believe that we're selfish. If we look closely, we can see how this belief influences our thoughts about others, as well as ourselves. For example, how do you feel when someone cuts you off while you're driving? What do you notice yourself thinking when someone doesn't keep an agreement or do what they said they would do? What thoughts do you have when you realize someone else wants something you also want?

If you're like me, your thoughts pit you against other people, making them into opponents or enemies. You might tell yourself that they're wrong or jerks (as I have done with drivers I didn't enjoy!). This thought pattern could also be described as the disposition of competition, of "me versus you." You might picture a football game as an archetypal, all-out version of this me-versus-you mentality. In a football game, there certainly isn't enough for everyone. There's only one small ball, and only one team is going to get it. Built into the structure of the game, there's the certainty of winners and losers.

These two ideas of scarcity and people's innate competitiveness work perfectly together. When I think about scarcity, I feel a sense of deflation, hopelessness, defeat, and despair. However, when I pair this thought with the idea that everyone, including me, is selfish and greedy, and that I need to go for what I want regardless of anyone else, I feel a sense of fire, drive, and confidence that I can do what it takes to get what I want or need. Wow, it's powerful! I actually feel like standing up and singing the national anthem, pronouncing that, "Yes, I can do this!" I believe the combination of assuming scarcity and greed is at the base of many of our social structures and ideologies, including nationalism.

Mary makes a final important point about these two assumptions: The reason we've been trained to believe in scarcity and greed is because these ideas make us afraid. If there isn't enough for us to thrive, we fear for our survival. And if we're all selfish and greedy and in competition with each other, we naturally feel afraid of others. Once we're afraid, we become easy to control, and we readily give our power to authorities that promise to protect us from each other and to help us get enough for our survival and well-being.

Mary clearly tells us, "You should always be cautious of anyone who supports ideas based on fear." This is valuable advice. We're constantly bombarded with all kinds of ideas. We need to use our discernment, based in our feeling-awareness, to evaluate the basis of these views. Are the ideas rooted in fear? Do the ideas create fear in those receiving the messages? Through awareness of the feelings communicated in a message and the feelings stimulated in response to it, we can choose which ideas we want to let into our consciousness.

Fear-based messages are usually employed to get us to agree to ideas and plans that others are proposing, often as part of a strategy to benefit the ones promoting the ideas. Mary sagely points out that our greatest danger doesn't come from lack of resources or the self-ishness or greed of others; it comes from accepting the very assumption that we're in danger and, on that basis, giving our power to others. Because we're powerful creators and capable of affecting reality, we actually create danger and negative outcomes by believing we're in danger and supporting those who promote this point of view.

Fortunately, we also have the power to create another paradigm, a paradigm of abundance based on the idea that there's enough for everyone. Mary equates abundance with the Sacred Feminine: "The Sacred Feminine assumes abundance, the infinite abundance of creative potential and ultimately the infinite abundance of the Divine itself." She then compares abundance to mother's milk. This moving image reminds me of the phrase "the land of milk and honey." It's natural for a baby to assume abundance, never doubting that milk will be available whenever the baby wants and needs it. Our natural state is to trust in an abundant world that provides for our needs and wants.

Yet, we also know that sometimes there isn't enough—whether it's milk for the baby or whatever else we want at a particular moment. That, according to Mary, is when we call upon the Sacred Masculine, the power of creative intelligence, to find a way to meet our needs. We need to be able to access both the Feminine and Masculine. We need to trust in the abundance of the world, and we need to be able to manifest through our mind, will, and intention. This is the Sacred Union of Feminine and Masculine.

Mary affirms the union of Feminine abundance and Masculine creativity: "You live in an amazing world of endless abundance, and you are incredibly powerful creators." Yet, many of us find the concepts of infinite abundance and ourselves as powerful creators of our reality hard to believe because they don't appear to be supported by our experience. And the strongest contradiction to these beliefs arises from our awareness of death. Once we understand that we will die, the ideas of limitation and lack seem to follow inevitably. We have only so much time, so many experiences, so many possibilities, and then it's all cut off by death—a death that may come far sooner than we would like or choose. Not only do we die, but all the people we love and depend on can die at any moment, too. Death looms as the ultimate limit, where all is taken away—and we seem to have little power to affect this.

Mary holds up a mirror so that we can see how that view is coming from our third-dimensional perspective. It looks like our world is limited, that people are selfish and greedy, and that everyone gets snuffed out in the end. But she says that she sees things very differently. Death is simply a change of state, like changing clothes or getting a new car. We don't "lose" our life at all. Death is really a transition to a new phase of our soul's journey. Nor does death end our relationship with anyone. We simply don't remember all this because, in this world, a veil of forgetting masks our awareness of our continuity after death.

Some people are able to see through this veil and are aware of the reality Mary describes. As more people awaken to our connectedness with all forms and states of life, the number of people experiencing the world like this will increase. I believe we're all moving toward this awareness, and the reality Mary depicts will ultimately become as obvious to all of us as our physical reality is now.

To help us broaden our perspective, Mary invites us to imagine what life would be like if there were no death. In response to her suggestion, I feel my survival fears unwinding and my belly relaxing. My immediate thought is that I wouldn't be worried that I'm not generating an income while I write this book! In such a world, I would no longer need to insure my survival through money or anything else. With the knowledge that I'm sustained, I would feel completely free to follow my heart's guidance as to what I choose to do with my life. Now I see what Mary is pointing to: we actually *are* sustained and we *are* free to create our life as our hearts lead us to do.

The third-dimensional realm could be characterized as "believing in separation," and death looks like the absolute separation from life. In describing the roots of that paradigm, Mary shows it to be a kind of catch-22: As long as we believe in the basic assumptions of lack, selfishness, and death as the ultimate loss, we'll keep creating the kind of reality that confirms those assumptions. Or, as Einstein put it, "No problem can be solved from the same level of consciousness that created it." Mary offers us a chance to move to a higher level of consciousness and to see things from her perspective. She encourages us to set aside our limiting beliefs, try out different ones, and see if they, indeed, produce the results she suggests they will.

Mary concludes by saying we all long for union, not only with our loved ones—both living and dead—but, really, with our whole self and with God. We long for union to heal us from our experience of separation in the third-dimensional realm. She suggests that many of us try to fill this desire for union through our intimate relationships, yet we're often disappointed because we're looking in the wrong place. Mary asserts that it's only our union with God and our whole self that will truly fulfill us. In that union, we will know ourselves as infinitely abundant because God is infinite and limitless. And because God is the Supreme Creator, we will know ourselves as infinitely creative manifestors. Then, as Mary tells us, "you will know that all is God, and you will enjoy that union through all your relationships and all your interactions. Every moment and circumstance will be a celebration of your union with God."

For me, that lands as supremely satisfying.

FIFTEEN

The Consciousness of Inclusion

Hello again, my dear ones ~

I will now speak to you further about the shift that you are in the midst of. It is the shift from relating to the world and to life as a place of lack and deprivation—where there isn't enough for everyone and you must compete with others to survive—into the knowingness of the world and life as abundant—where there is enough for all and all are sustained for as long as it is serving them to be here.

This is a shift that you are called to at this time. It is a profound shift in consciousness. It includes and affects so much. It includes your relationship to Earth, your mother in this realm. Earth is abundant, as you have seen for so long. Yet, of course, this does not mean that you will abuse her. Abundance consciousness leads to a different way of relating to others, including Earth.

When you are thinking in terms of lack and competition, it's "me versus them," and you need to focus on yourself and make sure you get enough. Since there isn't enough for everyone, focusing on others will be at your own expense.

Once you shift into abundance consciousness, you no longer need to think in terms of "me versus them" because there is enough for everyone. So along with this shift comes a new way of relating to others. You might call it "me *and* them," or "me *and* you." Instead of relating out of competition, now you're relating on the basis of inclusion. There is enough to care for everyone. And in this consciousness, you discover it is your joy to care for everyone. It is like being part of a family. You care for everyone within the family.

Part of what you're confused about in this disposition of inclusiveness is that it always includes you. Some of you have the incorrect idea that to care for others means not to care for yourself, to deny yourself so that you can focus on others. While this is partly coming out of a sincere yearning to care for others, it cannot happen at your own expense. Choosing one over the other is still subtly based in the consciousness of lack, only in this case you're choosing others over yourself. This is not the way the universe works. In truth, you always must be full yourself before you can give to others. Your giving to others comes out of your own fullness, your own abundance. Truly, it is God's abundance. That is what you are always giving. How can you give God's abundance to others if you yourself have not received it first? You are the vessel. It comes through you. Receive fully of God's abundance, and you will see how that naturally moves you to want to share this abundance with others.

Oddly, those who tend to hoard or to only think of themselves are doing so because they aren't actually receiving God's abundance. They must be helped to truly receive, not necessarily in the form that they're currently using. This is simply a substitute for their true nurturing, their true food, which is God. So they need to reconnect with their true Source. Then they will no longer want to hoard or to shut others out. God is joy, and it only increases our joy to share with others.

Support everyone, including yourself, in receiving fully of God's love and nurturing. Become full in God. And it will be natural to share this with others. You will share your light. You will share your love. You will share your wisdom. You will share your feelings. You will share your awareness of yourself and of life. You will share your heart's desires with others.

This is not the same as telling others what to do. All here have free will, and it is to be respected. Share yourself with others—your process in God. If you want to help others, share it as your desire to help, to contribute to them, and ask them if they would like to receive that. And respect their choice.

This is very difficult for most of you because you've been trained to think it's selfish to focus on yourself, your experiences, your feelings, and your desires. You've similarly been trained to think that it's higher or more loving to focus on others. Yet, you are God, and in denying yourself, you deny God. Knowing yourself and expressing that is to know and communicate your communion with God.

Others are God as well, and it is good to see them as such. And in this realm, part of each one's manifestation of God is their manifestation of free will. So part of honoring all as God is to respect each one's free will, to trust that individual's path in God, and to focus on your path and your life.

If you feel concerned about another, express that, but own it as your concern. You do not know what is right for them. You can ask them to change, but do not cross the boundary into force, based on thinking that you know what they should be doing. Respect their choice, and then choose what you will do. Remember your abundance, including your abundance of choices. You do not depend on others for your wellness. That comes from God. Don't confuse others as being your source. Your source is God.

The ultimate support is to support another in their path of connection with God. And you do not know what that is for another. Focus on your path, and ask God for guidance. Ask God for blessings for yourself and others, and give your trust to God. To try to control another—to think you are more competent than they are to make choices for them—is an act of not trusting God. You hurt yourself through your lack of trust. And it will always come back to you.

This is a fine distinction, yet so important. Do not suppress yourself by suppressing your caring and concern for others, as well as your desire for their support for your well-being. Yet, these must be owned as your own desires, rather than your ideas of what others should or must do. Express yourself as yourself, and listen to others in their own expression of their desires. See yourself and them as expressions of God, and respect everyone's free will to choose for themselves what they will do. If they are not choosing to cooperate with you in the way you had in mind, trust in the abundance of the universe, the abundance of God. You will be provided for, perhaps in a way that is so much more wonderful than the way that you were envisioning. Allow God to set your course. You steer the ship, but God sets the course.

I reach out to you in love and support on your journey in God.
I AM Mary Magdalene

*T*his message is a continuation of the ideas Mary introduced in the previous communication, "Lifting the Veil around Abundance and Death." In that talk, Mary discusses the assumptions of lack and competition for limited resources that underlie many people's way of relating to the world. Now, she illuminates another way of relating to life and the world, one based on abundance and the sure knowledge that we will be sustained.

Mary begins by saying that the shift into abundance and sustenance will affect many aspects of our lives, including how we relate to Earth. Assuming abundance, she reminds us, doesn't entitle us to exploit resources with no regard for the effects. Up until now, many of us have been doing exactly that, acting as though we can use and abuse Earth's treasures without taking responsibility for the consequences.

Providing for our own needs and desires at the expense of Earth means we're excluding Earth from our consciousness. Our lack of care for Earth is a symptom that we see ourselves as separate from her—it's us versus Earth. Mary describes the consciousness of inclusion as embracing all, which in this case means that we include Earth and Her well-being. This shift into inclusiveness is depicted by Mary as "me and you," not "me versus you."

Mary also compares inclusiveness to the operation of a healthy family, wherein everyone's needs are addressed when resources are distributed. For example, all members of a family are fed, clothed, and housed according to their needs instead of tending to some and not others. When we relate like this, we find it's joyful to care for everyone's needs.

I experienced this when I was living in a group household where we bought food and ate meals together. We shared the shopping and took turns preparing the meals. I remember what happy occasions our mealtimes were, and how delicious the food was, too. Later I moved into a group living situation where we all provided our own food and didn't eat together. I can still feel the sadness I felt in shifting into this arrangement, where I felt so much more separate from the others I was living with. I have often thought of Native American tribes or other indigenous people who share all that they receive and make sure that everyone is provided for, imagining how deeply this must affect their consciousness and relationship to life.

There's a direct link between assuming abundance and acting on the basis of inclusivity, where everyone's needs are considered. When we're in scarcity mode, the natural response is to beat out "the others" for limited resources. However, even if we're able to get what we need through competition, *if our gain occurs at the expense of others and their needs, we don't feel satisfied.* At some level we're aware we're actually connected to all, and so we feel disturbed when others' needs aren't met. The solution to this conflict lies in moving to a whole new level in consciousness, where we include everyone's needs and presume there's enough for all.

While most people agree with the *principle* of assuming abundance, many don't put it into action because it requires a deep level of trust in life and God. Living on the basis of abundance brings up questions: Will God actually sustain me, especially if I'm including everybody's needs as part of my needs? Is there really enough for everyone?

When I moved to Hawaii in 1999, I lived in a community that was dedicated to sustainability and staying connected to the Earth. After having spent most of my adult life indoors, suddenly I was immersed in a totally different lifestyle: we grew our own food, lived off-grid, and spent most of our time outside. One aspect of our living off-grid was that I was introduced to composting toilets, where all of our "humanure" was recycled into fertilizer for the food we grew. To my surprise, this had a profound effect on me. Suddenly, I understood that simply by eating and pooping and peeing, I was contributing to the earth that sustained me. I wasn't just a taker; I was giving back as well. I began to perceive myself as an inherent part of the circle of life, both contributing to this circle and receiving from it. I felt liberated by this insight—and quite joyful.

With this newfound sense of connection to the circle of life, I began to trust that I was meant to be here on Earth and would be sustained for as long as that was true. Staying alive wasn't something I had to struggle to achieve; it was part of how things flowed in the circle of life. By realizing this at a core level, I experienced a natural shift from *doing*, motivated by struggle, strife, and anxiety, to *being*, based on trust in the process of life. Along with this, I felt a sense of trust that when I was no longer meant to be here—when I had outgrown my present-life circumstance, learned my life lessons, and was ready to move on in my life journey—then I would be "recycled," my physical elements returning to the earth and my soul moving on to its new destination. From this perspective, I saw there really wasn't any possibility of loss of sustenance; even if I were to die, I would still be sustained in a new circumstance.

During that same time in Hawaii, I had a second insight that reinforced my developing sense of trust in sustenance. A significant part of our diet in the community consisted of fruit harvested from the land. Yet, I felt reluctant to eat the ripest, most attractive fruit. Instead, I felt that I should first eat the oldest fruit and save the newer fruit for later. A friend who had no qualms about eating the most attractive fruit available noticed this and found it quite humorous. Once he pointed out what I was doing, I realized I had "refrigerator consciousness." I was used to storing food in a refrigerator and portioning it out over a period of time so that the food would last until the next trip to the grocery store. But we weren't buying our food a week at a time and storing it in a refrigerator. We were eating what the earth provided every day. Even so, I still felt afraid to eat the best food immediately because that would mean letting the old food go and trusting that there would be new food tomorrow. I didn't trust that I would be provided for and that there would be enough.

Over time, as I watched my friend eat the best food and kept making my choice to eat the less-perfect, older food, I started to question my choice to deprive myself of the bounty of the moment in order to have security for the future. Eventually, although it took a significant leap of faith, I started to go for the best available food. In a tangible way, I was choosing to live in the "now" and to trust that I would be sustained in the future nows.

What happened? I never went hungry. I enjoyed my food much more. And I started to trust that life would sustain me in a whole new way. I realized my previous attitude hadn't really worked for me because I didn't enjoy relating to life on the basis of insecurity. The world became a kinder, softer place as I started to trust my ongoing sustenance. Instead of maintaining a sense of vigilance and opposition, I now started to enjoy the dance of "life and me together."

Mary points out another form of not trusting the abundance of life that is prevalent among spiritually oriented people: the belief that we need to take care of others at our own expense. When taken to the extreme, this belief leads to martyrdom. Putting others before ourselves might seem higher or more spiritual because it appears to be the opposite of focusing exclusively on our own survival, but this approach is still a form of "me versus you" and is based in lack and deficiency. In reality, there's enough for all of us. This understanding reminds me of the message communicated in the story of the loaves and the fishes.

Part of our spiritual work is to fill ourselves with the wholeness of God. Marshall Rosenberg emphasizes this concept when he uses the term *self-full*, rather than *selfish*: when we attend to our own needs, we become self-full. Since we all have an inherent need to contribute to others, taking care of our own needs inevitably will include giving to others. I've found the concept of self-full helps people see the natural importance of taking care of their own needs as a necessary part of caring for everyone's needs.

Mary puts this so clearly:

Support everyone, including yourself, in receiving fully of God's love and nurturing. Become full in God. And it will be natural to share this with others. You will share your light.

You will share your love. You will share your wisdom. You will share your feelings. You will share your awareness of yourself and of life. You will share your heart's desires with others.

Mary goes on to make an important distinction between giving to others and telling them what to do. She helps us to understand the interplay between the underlying spiritual principles: the principle of inclusion, which contains our need to contribute to others, and the principle of respect for everyone's free will. Although these precepts don't conflict with each other, it may take some skill to discern the difference.

Ultimately, respecting others' free will requires us to see other people as manifestations of God, just as we see ourselves as a manifestation of God. This isn't the same as thinking, *All is God, so I don't need to be concerned about other people or what they're doing.* That's independence. It's also not the same as thinking any particular person is God, so I should accept carte blanche whatever that person wants. That's dependence. Living interdependently means relating to all as God, so we're all to be respected for our freedom to create our reality. At the same time, we're all connected, which means we all share a desire for the well-being of everyone and we all affect each other.

Mary gives us some essential guidance on how to simultaneously hold and honor both respect for everyone's free will and care for everyone's well-being. Part of respecting other people's free will involves trusting their guidance from God.

For me, it's easy to fall into the trap of thinking that I know best. When I do, I put myself in the position of God. "I know best" is really a way of saying, "I know better." It's like saying that I've got the inside line to God and apparently the other person doesn't. When we think about this rationally, it's clearly not the case, yet at times many of us operate unconsciously from this assumption.

Why is this? When we were children, our parents seemed to know what was best for us, as did other authorities who told us what to do. Having been raised to believe in authorities, it's natural to assume that same orientation. Mary tells us we need to break the unconscious chain of dominance-subservience thinking in order to change this programming. Challenging this pattern begins with trusting that God is directing everyone's individual path and understanding that our job is to focus on ourselves and our choices. In Twelve-Step programs, this is called "staying on your side of the street." I've found that phrase a helpful reminder of what's mine and what isn't, a reminder of what to put attention on that supports me and what doesn't.

But the work doesn't stop there. We still have our need to help others, and we still feel affected by them. How do we engage others while staying on our own side of the street?

We do it by claiming our need to help as our own. Instead of telling others what they should or must do, we honestly own and express our need as being rooted in our desire to help or contribute to others. And then we ask if others would like our support and we listen to their response. If the response is no, we respect that and see how else we might meet our need to contribute to others' well-being. As Mary reminds us,

> Remember your abundance, including your abundance of choices. You do not depend on others for your wellness. That comes from God. Don't confuse others as being your source. Your source is God.

The ultimate form of help, Mary tells us, is always to support another in their path of connection with God. At the same time, we must remember that we don't know what that path is. Our recourse is to ask God for guidance and to ask for blessings for ourselves and others as we give our trust to the Divine. Mary's instruction is both wide and deep: she tells us how to be in relation to ourselves, others, *and* God. To do what she recommends, we need to surrender to God. When we are *directed by God*, we experience balance in supporting others in their path of connection with God while maintaining our own path. We remember that we don't know what is best for others, we ask blessings for all, and we respect everyone's free will.

Mary reminds us not to suppress our caring and concern for others or our desire to support them. Nevertheless, wanting to help doesn't mean that they should or must act according to our desires. Mary affirms this disposition in her final poetic instruction:

> Trust in the abundance of the universe, the abundance of God. You will be provided for, perhaps in a way that is so much more wonderful than the way that you were envisioning. Allow God to set your course. You steer the ship, but God sets the course.

I can't help but think that Mary is speaking from her own experience. I can only imagine what she felt when Yeshua was crucified and the process she went through in trusting God to provide for her and everyone. That awareness gives me profound inspiration and hope.

SIXTEEN

Opening the Heart

Greetings, beloved ~

Your heart is your most valuable organ. It is the key to your transformation. You have developed a protective barrier over your heart,
a wall or protective shielding. This is why it is so hard for you to
feel. It is also why it is so important for you to feel. Feeling will dissolve the wall and reopen your heart. And then your heart will be
able to continue its work in the evolution of your being.

The heart is the center of your being. It is your core. And
through the heart, all that you need will be activated. When the
heart is open and activated, it will allow your sacred heart to once
again come into union with your sacred mind and continue its
process of growth and opening in your soul's journey. Yet, you have
allowed your lower mind to dominate your heart. So your heart
has become sealed off through the domination of your thinking and
your refusal to feel.

Now is the time to turn this around. Learn to quiet your mind.
This can happen through meditation and prayer. And it also happens through feeling. When you feel, the mind naturally returns to
its right relationship in service to the heart. Feeling is a practice
you must engage because you have become trained not to feel.
Put your awareness in your heart and feel from your heart. Let

198 — MARY MAGDALENE BECKONS

your feeling-awareness expand out from your heart. And let yourself feel. Let your heart become the center of your being, the place you are residing and from which you are relating to the world. Feel from the heart. If you are in pain, feel it. Don't let your mind run away with thoughts of why this is happening, who did what that was wrong, and how you will fix it. Quiet the mind through engaging feeling.

When you have fully engaged your heart in feeling, then engage the mind to locate the source of the feeling. It will always be a beautiful quality, what I call a divine attribute. For example, your friend may have said something to you that was painful. Instead of focusing on the friend, how wrong they were, and what's the matter with them, focus on yourself. Specifically, focus on your feelings. Focus on your heart. What are you feeling in your heart? Are you feeling hurt? Let yourself fully feel it. Open to the hurt; fully be with it, viscerally and energetically. Merge with the hurt. It is you. Do not divorce yourself from your own experience. Be with it.

Then, when this full merging of feeling has occurred, bring in the mind. Ask yourself what is the source of your pain. Are you hurt because you're wanting care for your feelings? Or is it because you're wanting trust with your friend? Understanding? Support? Only you will know the true source of your feelings. And it will always be a beautiful quality, such as caring, trust, understanding, or support. If you have fully allowed yourself to merge with the feeling first, if you have fully given that process as much space and time as it needs to be full, then this second part of connecting with the source of your pain will bring about a shift. You will experience an opening, a peacefulness of connection with Source, with God, because you have connected with the root drive of union with the Divine. All your feelings are ultimately rooted in your connection with God. If you are in pain, it's not because of what someone else has done to you. It's because you have lost your connection with God. If you understand this, pain is an avenue of connection with God, and it will lead you to freedom, peace, and joy.

Do not be fooled by your mind. Do not waste your life meditating on how others are hurting you, how they are doing it wrong. If you notice yourself falling into that mind-set, let it awaken you in the moment. Use it as a red flag, telling you you've lost your connection to your heart. Reestablish that connection through feeling. Feel your pain, feel it fully, without avoiding it by going to your judgmental thinking. Be with the feeling and let it reopen your heart. And when that is full, use your mind to connect with the source, the beautiful attribute or quality that you are longing for. Now you will be able to feel the depth of your longing for that God-quality, and that longing will return you to peace, harmony, and openness to Source.

When that reconnection has occurred, there will be another shift. You will then be ready for movement, action. You may be energized and ready to take steps to make changes in your life. At that point, your mind will be ready to serve you by coming up with creative ideas that will support you in staying connected to the God-quality you are longing for. Or perhaps you will move into a kind of germination time where integration of all you've connected with can happen. This is movement, too, allowing the seed to sprout in its own timing.

Beloved, you have the ability to do this. You have all that you need. You simply must counter your own training that has taught you that this will hurt you. I tell you that this process of feeling will not hurt you. Indeed, it will absolutely help you. What you are doing now—meditating on the wrongness of others—is what is hurting you. It's keeping you a prisoner of your own mind, locked away from your heart. And your heart holds the key to all else, to all the doors to your higher awakening. You have the key. You simply must choose to use it.

*I love you and support you in your grand process
of awakening and growth in God.*
I AM Mary Magdalene

*I*n this message, Mary goes more deeply into two ideas: the primacy of our hearts and the necessity for feeling as the means of opening our hearts. She begins by telling us that we've developed a protective shield around our hearts that acts like a barrier to our feelings. I picture this as a castle or fortress with a stone wall around it.

The problem is, this wall around the heart that so many of us have erected isn't really doing what we'd hoped because barricading off our feelings doesn't actually protect us. We would be stronger if we had complete access to the valuable guidance our feelings offer us: our fear tells us to beware; our grief tells us that we need extra self-care and self-nurturing for healing; anger tells us we need to say no. If we really want to protect ourselves, one of the best things we can do is to stay connected to our feelings, not seal them off.

Many of us believe, at some level, that it's not safe to open to our feelings, especially our painful feelings. We're afraid that if we feel pain and invite it in, we'll suffer terribly or at least suffer more than we already do. This deep-seated fear comes from several sources. As children, we were often punished or ridiculed for expressing emotions; and when our role models avoided their own emotions, they communicated to us that feelings are dangerous. Perhaps even more significant, we experienced people acting upon their feelings in ways that resulted in others getting hurt, either physically or emotionally. It's essential to understand that *opening to feelings and allowing ourselves to fully experience them isn't the same as acting upon them.* Acting upon feelings, if done in an automatic, knee-jerk kind of way, is what I call reacting. It's separate from the act of experiencing the feeling.

Most of us who've been trained to avoid our feelings often don't notice our initial flash of emotion or the accompanying physical sensations. We've learned to instantly go into reaction mode and thus avoid experiencing the feeling. Our reaction might be to suppress the feeling and deny it, or we might impulsively act on the feeling—attacking or blaming if we feel anger, withdrawing if we feel fear, collapsing or giving up if we feel sorrow, or some other action we habitually gravitate to. Either one of these modes of responding—suppressing the feeling or reacting to it—is not the same as opening to the feeling and simply experiencing it. This distinction is critical; it's the difference between doing and being. Mary is calling us to being—to being with the feeling—rather than to doing.

Although we tend to believe opening to pain will result in increased pain, my own experience is just the opposite. I consistently find that opening to pain allows it to resolve. Avoiding pain, on the other hand, holds it in place. In other words, what we resist persists. The pain might persist in a different form. It might go into our bodies and persist as un-wellness or disease. It might persist as depression. It might persist as some kind of avoidance behavior—what we usually refer to as addictions. Energy is always conserved. Ignored feelings don't just vanish; they simply change form, and the form is usually not one that supports us. That's another reason why it is to our advantage to feel our feelings.

Mary assures us that opening to our feelings will not hurt us. In fact, what we're doing now—avoiding feeling and empowering our lower minds to take charge—is what is hurting us. When we seal off our hearts from our feelings, those feelings can't do their job of directing us to our inner divine qualities. Therefore, killing our feelings, at least in its effect, is similar to killing the messenger, which, as we know, doesn't solve the problem.

In addition, a whole other process is set in motion if we cut off from our feelings. Not only are we blocked from connecting with our inner bridge to God, we also create a void that our lower mind tries to fill. In the absence of the guidance of our feelings, our lower mind steps up to the plate and tries to direct us. But that's not what the mind is really good at. The result is that we become embroiled in endless thinking, a seeming rat-wheel of internal dialog, rehearsing over and over who or what did something wrong and telling ourselves what should happen. For many people, this has become a chronic state.

Mary states emphatically that we shouldn't waste our lives ruminating on what we think is wrong—whether it's thinking that others have wronged someone or thinking that we've done something wrong. Mary's directness in this statement reminds me of a hot knife cutting through butter. She tells us unequivocally not to waste our lives in the chaos of misplaced thinking. Instead, when we notice we're caught up in thinking about "who did what that was wrong," we should see it as a red flag warning us that we've lost our connection to our hearts.

Mary's perspective on the mind—specifically the lower mind, which some people call the monkey mind—isn't that it's an enemy that must be battled against; in the absence of the heart and feelings doing their jobs, the mind tries to help us. The mind is most beneficial when it is used in service to the heart. I find this statement not only compassionate, but also insightful and supportive. We don't need to oppose the mind. Rather, we need to make the heart fully functional and strong so that it can take the lead. To do this, we must bring down the wall around the heart. I'm reminded of the tearing down of the Berlin Wall that separated East and West Germany. What a celebration it was when the wall was opened! Mary is calling us to end our own internal cold war, to remove the iron curtain around our heart that keeps us from feeling and keeps our sacred heart and sacred mind from being in union.

How do we dismantle this wall? Mary explains that the first step is to quiet the mind. Two of the traditional methods for doing this are prayer and meditation. However, many people struggle with the discipline required for these practices. Others experience quietude during their practices of prayer and meditation, yet still experience the lower mind dominating their consciousness at other times. Because of these difficulties, I celebrate Mary's clarification that feelings provide another route for quieting the mind. When we feel fully, the mind naturally quiets. This path of feeling is the path of our inner Feminine, which complements the inner Masculine path of directing and mastering our mind.

Mary tells us specifically how to engage in the practice of feeling:

Put your awareness in your heart and feel from your heart. Let your feeling-awareness expand out from your heart. And let yourself feel. Let your heart become the center of your being, the place you are residing and from which you are relating to the world. Feel from the heart. If you are in pain, feel it. Don't let your mind run away with thoughts of why this is happening, who did what that was wrong, and how you will fix it. Quiet the mind through engaging feeling.

Mary says that we may need some time to experience what we're feeling, especially if we're not accustomed to it. Children will cry as long as they need to—often longer than adults are comfortable with, especially if the adults don't usually let themselves experience their own pain. Yet, children who are supported in taking as much time as they need to process their pain inevitably come to a place of peace and resolution. Telling a child to stop crying before that point simply aborts the process of reaching serenity and completion.

Once we've fully allowed the experience of feeling, we can then locate the source of that feeling, which will be one of our inner divine qualities, or attributes. The process of connection with those qualities can be illustrated by the experience of a woman I'll call Patty. Patty described to her friend the sadness she'd been feeling about her recent divorce from her husband. Her friend responded, "You're not sad, you're angry."

Several days after the interchange, Patty was still flooded with charged thoughts about her friend's remark. "I can't believe the way she's labeling me. She thinks she knows better than I do what I'm feeling. I don't need to justify myself to her. No one can understand what I'm going through. Now that her life is better, she doesn't remember what it was like for her when she went through this."

With help, Patty was able to access the feelings underneath all her thinking, and she realized she felt disturbed and hurt. As is often the case, each feeling signaled a different inner divine quality that needed attention. Her feeling of disturbance was related to her need for emotional safety in her friendships. She felt hurt because she deeply wanted empathy and support. Once she connected with these desired qualities of emotional safety, empathy, and support, a shift occurred. Mary describes this as the first shift. As Patty's previous thoughts subsided, along with her feelings of hurt and disturbance, she came to a newfound sense of peace and relief.

Patty's story illustrates Mary's assertion that our external circumstances aren't the cause of our pain. Nothing had changed about Patty's friend's remark. What changed was that Patty reconnected with her own inner divine qualities, her bridge to God. In this instance, the inner divine qualities were the qualities of emotional safety, empathy, and support. When Patty was able to connect to these beautiful qualities within her, she rediscovered her inner connection to God. And this brought her to peace. Reconnection with Source is our true desire.

We don't suffer from what someone else did to us or from any other outer event; nor do we suffer from the pain of our feelings. Ultimately, we suffer because we've lost our connection to God. Many of us think the way to relieve suffering is to "right the wrong" that's been done to us or to make the painful feelings go away. But those actions won't bring the relief we're seeking. Instead, we must reconnect with God because losing our connection to God is the source of our suffering. And our greatest ally in this process of reconnection is our feelings.

Even though a particular divine quality may not have been fulfilled in our outer lives, we always can connect with the fullness of that quality within. Our spiritual work is to return to our source of wholeness within through following our feelings. Once we reconnect with that wholeness, which is the wholeness of God, we return to peace.

From this place of peace within, a second shift occurs. At some point, a natural movement toward action takes place. Sometimes the action is to integrate the new understanding that's emerged. Most often, we want to engage in outward actions that support the inner divine qualities we've connected with. For example, in Patty's case, she might choose to talk with her friend about the feelings stimulated by the friend's comment and how those feelings are connected to her inner divine qualities—her needs for safety and empathy and support. She may then want to make a request of her friend, such as, "When you want to express ideas or intuitions about me, would you be willing to ask me first whether I want to hear your thoughts, and then ask me afterward how I feel about those thoughts?" What's most important in this part of the process is that our actions arise from our connection to the Divine. This connection frees our creativity to find new ways to align our world with Source.

To summarize, here are Mary's recommendations for opening the heart:

1. Notice if your mind is spinning with thoughts of yourself or others being wrong—or if you're defending yourself—and use those thoughts as red flags to inform you that you've lost connection to your heart.

2. Feel the feelings underneath the thoughts. If those feelings need time to be held and experienced, give them as much time and space as they need.

3. Allow the feelings to guide you to your inner divine qualities that need attention.

4. Rest in the peace of reconnecting with Source via your inner divine qualities.

5. Notice when you're ready to move into action, and take actions that will support the inner divine qualities you've connected with.

Mary closes by assuring us that we have the ability to follow these steps and regain access to our hearts. And our hearts hold the key to our higher awakening. I feel encouraged and clarified by both her instructions and her confidence in this process. As she proclaims, "You have the key. You simply must choose to use it."

SEVENTEEN

The Joy of Forgiveness

Hello, dear one ~

Many people today are speaking about forgiveness. And it is true: forgiveness is such an important process, especially at the stage where many of you find yourselves. Forgiveness will release you from the prison of thinking that someone else did something wrong to you or that you yourself did something wrong.

You see, your hurt is real. In this reality, this dimension, people really do get hurt. What you must understand is that this is different from thinking that someone has done something wrong. Wrong and right are simply fabrications of your mind, ideas that have been created to try to get people to do certain things that some people want them to do. Can you imagine living without the thoughts that some things are right or wrong? It is entirely possible and would benefit you tremendously.

If you didn't have the idea that something was wrong, you would simply be left with your hurt. This would support you in turning your attention to yourself and your own process rather than wasting your attention and energy on your thoughts about others. Then you could simply be with your hurt, giving yourself over to the process of feeling.

When you fully feel, no longer resisting with your mind or your busyness, but simply surrendering fully to feeling, you receive a gift. It may be a message, an understanding that realigns you to truth and opens your heart. Or you may simply be led to the beautiful quality, the divine attribute that is the source of your pain. And in reconnecting with that divine attribute, you will be led through the pain, all the way through, to the light at the end of the tunnel. Going through pain is like a kind of death, and in surrendering to it, you find the light at the end of the tunnel.

At this point, you can forgive because now your heart is open and you are at peace, once again reconnected to God. From this place, you can open your heart to the other. You can connect with their divinity, the beauty that was motivating them to do what they did, even if it may have caused you pain. You can open to them again in love. This is true forgiveness.

This will be followed by action, and you will know what action is appropriate for that particular circumstance. There is not one formulaic response that is necessary or best for engaging forgiveness. You will know in each circumstance what you're called to do. And it won't be difficult, like pulling teeth or climbing Mount Olympus. It will be easeful and joyful because the forgiveness has already occurred. This is simply the natural outcome, the action flowing out of that new alignment, that shift at the heart.

Sometimes you may communicate with the person. Sometimes you may not. Sometimes you may ask for their forgiveness. Sometimes you may choose to have less to do with that person. Sometimes you may see how this circumstance served you, even if it created pain. Sometimes you may see how you created this circumstance. If it is true forgiveness, you will feel the unity of your heart and soul with this person.

Forgiveness is a hugely liberating practice. It can be engaged daily. Do not confuse it, however, with denying pain or denying that you experienced hurt. Do not confuse the practice of forgiveness with the idea of forgiveness or other related ideas such as, "I created this myself," or "There's only oneness, so not to forgive is only hurting me," or "This is just an illusion," or "I *should* forgive this." While ultimately those statements are true, holding them as ideas will not help you and will actually hurt you if you're using the ideas to avoid feeling the pain.

The process of forgiveness must be engaged through feeling. That is the corridor that will lead you to your open heart—your light-filled room of wonder, love, and peace—and your heart's joy. Take that path, dear one, and reunite with your true Beloved. In that vastness of joy, you will have more than enough excess to love the one who has hurt you, to embrace and hold that one in this heart-full unity.

I love you and call you to join me in this space of divine union.
I AM Mary Magdalene

*I*n this communication, Mary guides us to move beyond "right" and "wrong" through the practice of forgiveness. She describes this process as releasing us from the "prison of thinking that someone else did something wrong...or that you yourself did something wrong." I love her image of right-wrong thinking as a jail and her message that we can release ourselves from this self-imposed imprisonment. This analogy contains a subtle irony: A prison is a place for isolating those who society judges as having done something wrong. But here, Mary suggests that those who do the judging are the ones who are actually imprisoned and isolated.

Right-wrong thinking is a hallmark of third-dimensional consciousness, but in the fourth dimension, we begin to transcend this form of duality. Accordingly, Mary's instruction for forgiveness can be viewed as a fourth-dimensional practice. When she presents the possibility of living without the ideas of right and wrong, she's calling us to imagine what life in the fourth dimension and beyond is like.

Mary clarifies the difference between judging something as right/wrong, good/bad, etcetera, and acknowledging that it has affected us or others. She's not giving us an idealistic formula for how to live, telling us to simply love and accept everything. Rather, we need to discern the difference between thinking and feeling. We can let go of thinking that someone is wrong or right and engage our feeling as to how the action affected us. Instead of labeling the person or event as good/bad, appropriate/inappropriate, acceptable/unacceptable, etcetera, we can focus on ourselves and our own feeling-experience.

Focusing on our own experience is clearly different from asserting—as some spiritual teachings propose—that an action had no effect upon us: "If you were really spiritual, this wouldn't affect you." To deny that events affect us is simply to suppress our experience, which will result in shutting down our spiritual connection to life. I think this understanding is worth reiterating: Mary doesn't ask us to deny our experience of being affected by others and events. Rather, she's telling us we can choose to perceive experience through our faculty of feeling rather than misguidedly channeling it into thoughts of rightness or wrongness about others. Redirecting judgments into feeling is the beginning of the process of forgiveness.

I want to summarize at this point because these differentiations are so important, yet they can be easy to miss when we're on the slippery slope of reacting to something painful. The first part of the forgiveness process is:

1. Notice and acknowledge that something has affected you.

2. If you find yourself judging the event or person as wrong, bad, inappropriate, and so forth, notice you're doing that and redirect your energy into step 3 below.

3. Experience your own feelings as they arise.

I'd like to pause here to expand a bit on the third step, which directs us to experience our own feelings. Our feelings are comprised of emotions and physical sensations; examples of feelings are feeling hurt, powerless, sad, afraid, tense, worried, doubtful, and so forth. The tricky part here is, because we've been trained to think in terms of judgments rather than feelings, we sometimes say, "I'm feeling..." and then follow with a judgment. For example, someone may say, "I'm feeling abandoned" or "I felt betrayed," but neither of these statements expresses feelings. They're actually thoughts about what someone else has done to you. If you're thinking that you've been abandoned, you might actually be feeling fear or sadness or loneliness. If you're thinking that someone has betrayed you, you might feel anger or powerlessness.

Another example of thoughts masquerading as feelings occurs when we make statements such as "I feel that this is nit-picking" or "I feel like this has all been for nothing." Again, both statements are expressions of thoughts rather than feelings. In the first example— "I feel like this is nit-picking"—we might be feeling annoyed or impatient. In the second example—"I feel like this has all been for nothing"—we might be feeling despair. The same thing occurs when we say, "I feel..." followed by a pronoun or a noun—"I feel she is manipulative." In this case, the feeling might be caution or resentment.

A few guidelines can help us in discerning between thoughts and feelings. The first is that feelings are our own, and we experience them internally. Feelings aren't about what others have done, even if their actions stimulated the feeling. The second is that feelings are both emotions and visceral sensations. They're actually sensory data, something that we *feel* (thus the term *feeling*). This may seem ridiculously obvious, and it would be if we hadn't been trained to cut off from our feelings and focus on our thoughts. Many of us are now unlearning that training and relearning how to feel.

This process of experiencing our feelings may take some time, especially if we're in the habit of holding back or repressing our feelings. We can justify avoiding this work by telling ourselves we don't have the time or that once we open to our feelings, we'll never find our way out. But feelings naturally resolve when we give them space and time. The process is like the healing of a wound; it takes time, and it naturally leads to health and wholeness.

In reality, we actually save time by allowing our feelings to express themselves. Repressed feelings often cost us more than time by causing depression, sickness, anger, or aggression. They also cause us to do things poorly and inefficiently because our "heart isn't in it." If we're not used to experiencing our feelings, initially we may need to devote extra time to learning to do so as we build up our atrophied "feeling-muscles." Eventually, the time spent experiencing feelings will be less than the time spent dealing with the consequences of blocking feelings. When we allow our feelings to surface and resolve, we experience an increase in energy that makes us much more productive and better able to use the rest of our time.

Once we fully allow ourselves to experience what we're feeling, we'll receive a gift. The gift may take the form of a message or new understanding, or it may be our reconnection with God through our inner divine qualities. Mary likens this process to finding the light at the end of the tunnel and says that going through pain is a kind of a death-rebirth process. Since I'm still retraining myself to allow and embrace my feelings, engaging this process can at times feel like being lost in a dark tunnel. That's why Mary's analogies resonate with me. As I receive the gift of allowing my feelings, I feel as though I'm emerging once again into the light. Remembering this analogy inspires me to continue forward "into the light" through the seeming darkness of experiencing pain.

After we've allowed our feelings to bring us their gifts of understanding, peace, and reconnection with God, we're then ready to focus on the other person. Mary describes this as opening again in love to the other. Even though the other person's actions caused us pain in some way, when we connect with the inner divine qualities that were motivating that individual, we can see the beauty behind the actions. We can love the source, the person's heart-intention, even if we don't like the way the person tried to fulfill their inner divine qualities. Understanding the other's motivations is what allows us to authentically love another while still remaining connected to the feelings and inner divine qualities stimulated in us as a result of that person's actions.

A friend asked me to help him by facilitating a healing with a work associate he'd had a falling-out with. When I declined his request and gave him the reasons for my refusal, he became angry with me, insisting, "I would do that for you if you had asked. After all these years we've been friends and all the things I've done for you, I can't believe you're not willing to do this one thing for me."

His response was very challenging for me, and I became aware of a swarm of judgmental thoughts spinning in my head: *What a self-centered, demanding person he is! He isn't even interested in me and what's going on with me that's preventing me from doing what he's asking. All he wants is to get his way. And he assumes that he knows what's the right thing to do and that I should just lie down and do whatever he says rather than decide for myself what's best for me. He obviously has some lessons to learn, and that's clearly why this is happening to him in the first place.*

Rather than continuing down that path of turbulent thoughts, I chose to go into my feelings. First, I realized that I felt scared because my friend was being extremely forceful in trying to get me to do what he wanted. He showed this through his tone of voice, his unrelenting stance that he was right and I should do what he wanted, and all the reasons he presented about why I was wrong. I needed emotional safety—to be able to say my truth and be accepted. I also felt shocked at how he was treating me because I wanted to be respected for my choices about what I was or wasn't willing to do, especially by a friend. Finally, I felt hurt because my inner divine quality of being treated with care wasn't getting fulfilled. My need for care was probably the deepest and most important of all the beautiful qualities I'd connected with. The others—for emotional safety and respect for my choices—were important, too, but they came from more superficial layers in my heart.

Once I connected with my inner divine qualities, I was naturally able to experience those qualities in their fullness. As I drew from my internal wellsprings of emotional safety, respect, and care, I felt myself once again connected with Source. From there, I effortlessly rested in the peace of union with God.

I was now ready to shine the light of my attention back on my friend. What was motivating him? I could see that he was scared and feeling desperate for support, and that underneath he wanted to be understood by his work associate and to have peace in that relationship. I could feel that I authentically wanted him to have all of those inner divine qualities—support, understanding, and peace. Although I wasn't enjoying the way he was trying to satisfy his inner beautiful qualities, I could connect with the beauty in him that was at the source of his actions. And by doing so, I could feel love for him and forgive him for his actions. I didn't agree with his choices or condone them; I didn't change my mind about choosing not to do what he was asking. I simply returned to love—for him and for me.

At this point, when our hearts have reopened to ourselves and the other, we are ready to choose how we would like to act. And the choices are truly infinite. Forgiveness is not about becoming a doormat. We are cocreators. Once we've moved into authentic love for ourselves and the other, we can choose what we will do. We may express forgiveness or we may ask to be forgiven. We may choose not to communicate. We may ask for different actions in the future. Or we may choose to have fewer interactions with that person while still staying in the disposition of love and blessing. *Because we've already forgiven,* whatever actions we choose will be easeful. The actions flow naturally from forgiveness instead of being difficult and effortful because they stem from a sense of righteousness or a *should*. Mary compares forced forgiveness to climbing Mount Olympus or pulling teeth! She tells us, "If it is true forgiveness, you will feel the unity of your heart and soul with this person."

In the situation with my friend, as soon as I forgave him, I immediately thought of another way I could support him that would also work for me. I e-mailed him and described the emotions stimulated in me by his response, along with the inner divine qualities at the heart of those emotions. I apologized for my initial defensiveness, explaining that I had reacted because I'd been disconnected from my emotions and inner divine qualities. I then told him I had come up with another way that I could support him, which was to offer him a healing session so he could process his falling-out with his work associate. I felt grateful for all the inner work I had done and the love and inner peace I'd come to—which included self-love and loving forgiveness for my friend—and the new vista of possibility that had opened up for me as a result.

Mary concludes by saying, "Forgiveness is a hugely liberating practice." She says we can engage in forgiveness as a daily practice. And she once more reminds us that to forgive does not mean distracting ourselves from our experience or our pain through spiritual ideas like "I created this myself," "There's only oneness, so not to forgive is only hurting me," "This is just an illusion," or "I *should* forgive this." She affirms that while there is some truth in those statements, if we are using the ideas to avoid feeling pain, this kind of thinking doesn't support us. As she says so beautifully,

> The process of forgiveness must be engaged through feeling. That is the corridor that will lead you to your open heart— your light-filled room of wonder, love, and peace—and your heart's joy. Take that path, dear one, and reunite with your true Beloved. And in that vastness of joy, you will have more than enough excess to love the one who has hurt you, to embrace and hold that one in this heart-full unity. I love you and call you to join me in this space of divine union.

If I weren't already convinced of my desire to follow the path of forgiveness, this message would certainly tip the scales. Mary's few words, like a melody playing in my soul, once again speak deeply to my heart. I find myself effortlessly responding from the depths of my being, naturally drawn to reuniting with my "true Beloved" and grateful for all of Mary's skillful help in this process.

PART V

The Greatness
beyond the Mind

EIGHTEEN

Choosing the True God

Hello, again ~

I come to you today with a message about blame. I have talked about this before, but I am choosing to say more about it because it is such a rampant pattern in your society at this time.

Blame is an activity of separation. It is attributing your feelings, your pain, to something outside of yourself, saying that it caused you to feel this way. You might say, "So-and-so is the cause of my pain," or "I feel this way because of what so-and-so did." You are attributing wrongness to the party that you're blaming. In doing this, you are setting yourself up as their judge, the one who knows what's right and wrong, the one who knows better than the party you're blaming. You are setting yourself up as superior, with superior knowledge or wisdom. You are setting yourself up as God.

Yet, this is not the true God. This is the god of separation. And in ascribing to this god, you are actually separating yourself from the true God.

God does not judge. God has no need of judgment. God is love and unity. You have been told by some that you will be judged by God at the end of your lifetime and either rewarded by being sent to heaven or punished by being sent to hell. But this is not accurate. At the end of your life, you will review your own life through your higher self, along with your loving guides, to see what lessons you fulfilled and what you still need to learn. This is for your help in continuing on your soul's journey of spiritual evolution. It is not to give you a reward or punishment. You do not need a reward or punishment. No one does. You are inherently motivated toward union with God because your soul remembers that bliss, that ecstasy, and continually longs for it in the depth of your being.

Judging others through blame and criticism takes you away from that bliss, that ecstasy. Can you feel that? How happy do you feel when you blame others, criticize them, and say that they are the cause of your unhappiness? You are always free to be happy in every moment. It may take some growth in consciousness for you to realize this and make use of it, but, in truth, you always have access to happiness. It is because you always have access to God. You are simply believing that you don't. That is the cause of your unhappiness—your own beliefs, not what someone else has done.

Pain does not need to make you unhappy, because it does not need to separate you from God. You choose to separate yourself by not feeling your pain, and then you blame your experience on another, or your circumstances, or your government, or your health, or the weather, or whatever! Your mind can create endless reasons why you're the victim, why it's someone or something else's fault. Do not believe this. It's a downward spiral into endless suffering. This is your true hell, not something that happens after you die.

You always have a choice. If you're habituated to blaming others for your pain, make the choice to own your pattern. Notice that you're doing that, and be honest with yourself about it. And then make the next choice to stop blaming others. Just be with your pain. And continue to be with it. Merge with it and notice what happens.

You will probably be surprised. It will lead you to peace, to openness, to happiness. This is so, even if the pain doesn't go away. Your own openness has led you to reunion with God.

Blessings to you, dear one, in the love and light of God.
I AM Mary Magdalene

*M*ary begins this message by saying, "Blame is an activity of separation." I'm fascinated by how, in this one concise statement, Mary gets to the very heart of the activity of blame. When we blame, we separate ourselves from our own experience—usually an experience of pain—by projecting our awareness outward onto someone else. Instead of staying connected to ourselves and our experience, we distance ourselves by focusing on the person we claim caused our pain. Specifically, we focus on their *wrongness* in creating pain for us.

Most of us don't even notice how blame separates us from our own experience. We move so quickly into thoughts about who did something to cause us pain that we generally miss the experience of the pain itself. That movement outward into blame serves a purpose: it protects us from feeling pain.

I remember an incident that dramatically and poignantly brought this home for me. I was getting into my friend's car with her eight-year-old son. The boy accidentally closed the door on his finger and immediately felt immense pain. The first words out of his mouth, which he said with great vehemence, were, "Stupid car!" Several seconds later when he could no longer contain the pain, he reluctantly began to cry.

Obviously, the car wasn't stupid, and the boy's statement had very little to do with his actual experience. I understood his anger as a defense against feeling the anguish he was in. Fortunately, he was still connected enough to his real feelings that he was able, with a slight delay, to allow his authentic response.

Sadly, many of us never get to the point he reached of opening to our feelings. Through our deeply ingrained pattern of using blame to avoid pain, we hold our awareness that we're in pain at bay, and we're similarly unaware that we've opted to blame rather than experience our pain. By pointing all this out to us, Mary supports us to become conscious of what we're doing, thereby giving us the opportunity to make a different choice.

When we blame others, we put ourselves in the position of judge and God, declaring the other as being at fault and the cause of our suffering. Clearly, this distances us from the other person. Yet, there's an even more important effect of maintaining a position of superiority over others. The judging god we're presuming ourselves to be isn't the true God. In fact, Mary calls it the god of separation. By clinging to this god, we alienate ourselves from the real God, who doesn't judge. Mary clarifies that "God has no need of judgment. God is love and unity."

This view of God as nonjudgmental stands in contrast to what some religions teach: that God will judge us when we die, and we will either be rewarded by being sent to heaven or punished by being sent to hell. Mary tells us this isn't so. Once again, she paints a picture of a different kind of world. Not only is it a world without concepts of right and wrong, it's also a world without a judging God—and no heaven and hell to reward or punish us.

I imagine this raises questions for people who believe in the necessity of an external system of moral authority and enforcement: What will cause people to act with love, kindness, compassion, and integrity instead of hurting others? If there's no right and wrong, no good and bad, no judgment, and no heaven and hell, won't our world become a chaotic, destructive, free-for-all, with murder, rape, and pillage as the order of the day?

Mary answers these questions by saying we don't need reward and punishment because we're inherently motivated toward union with God. We've already experienced that union, and in our souls, we remember it as blissful and ecstatic. In the depths of our being, we continually long to re-create this state.

The idea that people require judgment, along with reward and punishment, comes from the premise that humans are solely motivated by self-survival and the drive for base pleasure. If we are only out for ourselves, then we require external control to insure we don't kill and injure each other. Concepts of right and wrong and a system of authority to mete out rewards and punishments are just such instruments of control.

Mary's point of view is radically different. Rather than seeing humans as rising up—and not very far—from the primordial muck of lower life forms with lower consciousness, she tells us we've already known the bliss and ecstasy of union with God. We began in total union with God and have gradually descended over lifetimes into increasingly lower dimensions of reality so that God could experience itself in these more concrete forms. Mary says that in our souls we still remember that greater union with the Divine. In fact, that memory is the primary driving force motivating us to continue to grow and evolve in ways that once again embody that state of grace.

I have memories of having lived in ways that were more loving and more blissful and ecstatic, which I believe are memories of having lived in greater union with the Divine. Earlier in my life, I tended to dismiss and suppress these memories because they weren't validated by others or the mainstream culture in which I lived. Nonetheless, in recent years, these memories have become clearer as I've given myself permission to access and believe them. While not everyone may remember this state of union as clearly as I do, I think many people have a vague sense of other possibilities; this may appear in dreams, fantasies, imaginings, through resonating with stories that depict more loving or expanded possibilities, or just from a general impulse or urge to another way of living and being that they deeply believe is possible.

Along with offering us a more uplifting view of what motivates us in life, Mary gives us an inspiring vision of what happens when we die. She tells us it's actually our higher self and our loving guides who do our life review to see if we accomplished the goals and lessons we agreed to prior to incarnating—and to clarify what we want to take on for our next lifetime. This life review is quite different from being judged and then rewarded or punished. It's actually a form of help and loving guidance to keep us moving forward on our soul's path. Our life review is also not something happening to us from an outer authority; it's an intrinsic process, a process we engage relative to ourselves that supports us in our return to the bliss and ecstasy of union with God.

I see many commonly held beliefs about heaven and hell as mistaken interpretations of the concept that we create our reality and consequently experience the effects of our consciousness now. As Mary says, "Your mind can create endless reasons why you're the victim, why it's someone or something else's fault. Do not believe this. It's a downward spiral into endless suffering. This is your true hell, not something that happens after you die."

In other words, when we blame others for our experience and put ourselves in the victim position, we suffer the results of our activity in the present; this is our self-created hell. Mary takes her statement further by asking us to notice how we feel when we blame and criticize others. Do we feel happy? She tells us that blame and criticism take us away from the bliss and ecstasy of communion with God, which is the source of our happiness.

However, when we release our habits of judgment and blame, we create a different reality, one that's more connected to God's delight and love. Mary clearly states, "You are always free to be happy in every moment. It may take some growth in consciousness for you to realize this and make use of it, but, in truth, you always have access to happiness. It is because you always have access to God." That's really quite radical—and potentially liberating. Just as we can create our hell, or separation from God, in any moment, we also have the opportunity to create our heaven through the happiness of connecting with God.

Mary goes on to say that if we're not experiencing happiness in any moment, it's because we believe we don't have access to God and happiness. Our beliefs are the real source of our unhappiness—not what someone else or the world is doing to us. For most of us, the belief that we're cut off from God is so constant and ongoing that most of the time we're not even aware of it. When a painful situation arises, however, we're suddenly on overload; the pain of the moment, along with our ongoing, chronic pain of separation, is too much, and we have a kind of explosion outward. We discharge the pressure by blaming something external to ourselves.

Mary concludes her message by reiterating that pain doesn't need to take us away from our happiness. In fact, it can be an avenue of reconnecting us to God because we can connect even more deeply than we could prior to the pain. She tells us to make the choice to stop blaming others and instead choose to feel and merge with our pain—and she tells us once more that we'll probably be surprised at the result. We'll experience peace, openness, and happiness, even if the pain doesn't go away. Why? Because we're returned to union with God.

In her usual manner, Mary has brought her discourse around to union with God, which I see as her greatest love and truly all she really wants to focus on. Her devotion to God is contagious—the more I read and reread her words, the stronger it becomes in me. I believe that is what she most desires.

NINETEEN

The Great Freedom

Greetings to you, my dear one ~

I would like to speak about Yeshua, my most beloved partner. I want
to take you with me to the time that he was judged as being a traitor
and was condemned to his death. You have heard about this through
your stories and records of his life. What I wish to draw your attention to is his response. He did not defend himself. He did not argue
with his captors or those who wanted to suppress him. He did not
try to prove their wrongness. He stayed with his truth, the truth of
who he knew himself to be. He forgave those who were hurting him
and asked for their forgiveness from God.

He certainly could have argued. Yeshua was the most brilliant
being on Earth. His mind carried the brilliant light of God. But he
did not use that light to try to suppress others, even others who were
hurting him. He used that light to stay connected with God and to
invite others to join him in that light. He was absolutely clear about
his purpose, and his physical pain could not deter him from it. The
light carried him beyond pain, beyond clinging to that lifetime. He
knew his immortality in God, his oneness with God.

And this is what you are called to as well, dear ones. Do not let
your pain deter you from your union with God, your union with
your own heart. Every pain, even the smallest one, is a test and an

227

opportunity. Will you believe your physical, third-dimensional reality and fight the pain as if it were a dragon trying to slay you? Or will you see it as yet another manifestation of God, an opportunity for union?

This is not to say that you will never act, that you will be merely passive. It's that you wait to act until you are in union with God, and you let your action be directed by God. Then you are free, already free in God, and your action is God's play, however serious it may appear.

This is the great liberation, the freedom of your soul. No one and no thing can take it away, regardless of what happens to you. May you know this freedom.

In deepest love,
I AM Mary Magdalene

*T*his is one of Mary's simplest messages, yet the profundity of it moves me at my core each time I read it. Partly, I'm affected by the bittersweetness of Mary speaking of her life with Yeshua and transmitting the depth of her love for him. And, partly, I appreciate the simplicity of the message itself and the great truth I find in such few words.

Mary begins with taking us to the time that Yeshua was judged a traitor and asks us to focus on Yeshua's response. Yeshua didn't judge those who had judged him. He didn't defend his rightness, nor did he try to convince his captors of their wrongness. He held to the truth of who he knew himself to be, and he chose to forgive. Yeshua's silence didn't mean that he was incompetent or lacking in mental prowess. Mary describes him as the most brilliant being on Earth because "his mind carried the brilliant light of God."

The next part of her communication is what makes this message so powerful for me. Mary says that Yeshua chose to use the light of his mind to stay connected to God and to invite others into that light. He did this instead of using the light to try to avoid pain—*and the light carried him beyond pain.*

We all have the opportunity to use pain to connect us to God. If others judge us, misrepresent us, or even intentionally try to hurt us in some way, we usually experience pain. What inspires me in Mary's description is the image of our mind as carrying the light of God. I picture the mind as a lighthouse, and we can choose where we focus the beam. Will our focus be on the rightness or wrongness of those involved? Will we try to protect ourselves from feeling pain? Or will we use the light of our minds to connect with God and spread the light?

Mary reports that Yeshua was "absolutely clear about his purpose, and his physical pain could not deter him from it. The light carried him beyond pain, beyond clinging to that lifetime. He knew his immortality in God, his oneness with God." If we were that clear about our immortality in God and oneness with God, I believe we would live very differently. Nonetheless, Yeshua's sureness and awareness speak to our hearts—even two thousand years after his death. We have known this same certainty of our oneness with God in the past, but because of the veil of forgetting we experience in the third dimension, we don't consciously remember it now. I can't prove our previous experience of divine union with my mind, but I feel it in my heart response to Mary's depiction of Yeshua.

Mary reveals that "every pain, even the smallest one, is a test and an opportunity. Will you believe your physical, third-dimensional reality and fight the pain as if it were a dragon trying to slay you? Or will you see it as yet another manifestation of God, an opportunity for union?" In other words, will I let my pain throw me off the path of union with God? Will I let the pain become my enemy and spend all my energy combating it? Or will I allow the pain to draw me deeper into my heart, deeper into the union with the Divine that I access through my heart?

Mary finishes by reminding us that she's not asking that we stoically endure our pain. She tells us to unite with God first, and then let God direct what we do. When we do this, we are free, and our action is God's play. In the Hindu tradition, this is called *lila*, or the play of God. Mary calls it "the great liberation, the freedom of the soul."

Whatever we call this freedom, it sounds divinely attractive. I give deep thanks to Mary for opening the window of her profound understanding of Yeshua and for her tremendous help in supporting all of us to live the great liberation of our souls.

TWENTY

Releasing Guilt and False Responsibility

Greetings, beloved ~

Dear one, I want you to know that we are always here with you. You can never lose your connection to us, unless you choose to turn away. Whenever you open and ask for us to be with you, we are here. We are always loving you and always most present for you. Such are the bonds of love and light that we have with you. It is beyond space and time, as you know it. Your sense of time is not the same as ours. You may turn away for a space of time, but we are always here and always with you, available for you. We love you, and that does not change.

Do not have guilt if you have not been open to us for a time. Guilt is the contrivance of your own mind. We do not want it for you, nor do we ask it of you. We only want you to open to love and light. That is our great joy and desire, what we support you in. You can choose that in any moment. There is never any limit upon that, no barrier or obstruction. It is always available to you.

The obstruction is in you, dear ones—in your thinking, in your physical bodies, in your emotional bodies, in your energy bodies. This is why it is necessary to cleanse and purify these bodies, so that you can be open to light and love.

You have never done anything wrong or bad. Thinking that

you've done something wrong or bad is just more obstruction in the mind, and therefore you feel guilt or shame. Really, all you are ever doing is opening to light and love or turning away from it.

You have not done anything wrong because another feels pain as a result of your actions. Pain is part of this dimension in which you reside. You do not create it or cause it. You are not that powerful. Pain is here to help you grow and open in light and love. It is your ally in this realm of density. If another is in pain, do not deny them their opportunity for growth and opening to light and love.

Loving another is not the same as taking responsibility for their pain. Their pain is theirs, part of their spiritual journey. To love another is to allow them their pain and to love them in the midst of it. You can support them if they choose that, and if it is for your highest good, but you cannot remove their pain, nor is it your responsibility to do so. To love another is to experience their pain with them, to be fully present for their pain, and to love and open in the midst of that.

This is what I did with Yeshua. I could not remove his pain, nor was it my responsibility to do so. He chose his spiritual path, and mine was to love him and be fully present, heart wide-open to him in his glory and his pain. This is part of the journey of light and love in this dimension.

This is not an easy place. It is a place of pain, and pain is inherent to the spiritual path in this realm. Still, it is always in your highest good to open to light and love, which means opening to pain in this realm. Ultimately, you will transcend the pain and be moved on in light and love. Neither you nor anyone else knows when that will happen. It happens again and again in moments, for periods of time. At some point, it will happen more permanently. Until then, your path is the same as it has always been, which is to open to light and love. In this realm, that will include pain. But it is the only path that truly satisfies.

My message to you is simple and always the same: Stay true to light and love. Open yourself fully to light and love. Let light and love be your guide. You will know you are doing this by your peace, by your openheartedness, by your radiance. And as you do that more and more, we will always be with you, supporting you on your path home to light and love.

We welcome you, dear ones, with joy and anticipation.
I AM Mary Magdalene

*B*efore receiving this communication, I had been out of town for several days and had taken a break from receiving channeled messages. After resuming my daily communications with Mary, I felt as if I'd done something wrong, and I was afraid she might be angry and might even stop communicating with me.

Mary begins by directly responding to my guilt and my fears of losing contact with her: "I want you to know that we are always here with you. You can never lose your connection to us, unless you choose to turn away. Whenever you open and ask for us to be with you, we are here." She makes the clear statement that higher beings aren't going to abandon us, regardless of our choices. We can lose our connection to them only if we turn away and thus cut off the connection. But as soon as we return, the connection is available to us because they never left. Her words served as a potent antidote to my self-flagellating thinking.

In responding to my perception that I'd been incommunicado for a *long* time, Mary explains that we in the third dimension perceive time differently than beings in the higher realms. While we may sense a significant period of time has transpired, for those in the higher realms, no separation has occurred, either in space or in time. I can't say that I fully understand this idea, but it opens my mind to a much broader perspective, including the possibility that the way I perceive time may be extremely limited.

Mary goes on to describe guilt as a purely mental creation, emphasizing that higher beings don't ask us to feel guilt or want us to. Instead, they want us to experience light and love, which are available to us in any moment. It's only the obstructions in our bodies, emotions, minds, and energy that block us from experiencing them. In the case of guilt and shame, the obstructions are in the mind. When we feel guilt, we tell ourselves that we've *done* something wrong; with shame, we think we *are* wrong or bad. Guilt is about our actions; shame is about who we are. Both involve pointing the finger of "wrongness" or "badness" at ourselves.

The bottom line is this: if we want to feel light and love, we must release the obstructions that block them. We can let go of guilt and shame by releasing our concept of wrongness or badness. Mary unequivocally states: "You have never done anything wrong or bad...all you are ever doing is opening to light and love or turning away from it."

My true feelings—as opposed to my feelings of guilt and fear, laced with self-judgments that I'd done something wrong—were a mixture of sadness about not having connected with Mary for several days and confusion about how to support myself in other ways (such as having fun and adventure through traveling) while still maintaining my connection to Mary. I realized the inner divine qualities at the source of my feelings were both my longing to maintain my connection with Mary and my need for clarity about how to attend to some of my other inner divine qualities, such as fun and adventure.

Through connecting with the source of my feelings, I experienced a shift into peace about the situation. I once again returned to my sense of wholeness within myself and oneness with the Divine. I no longer judged myself for doing something wrong, and I didn't feel conflicted. From this peaceful place, an understanding arose—seemingly of its own accord—of other choices I could have made that may have worked better for me. For instance, I could have told Mary about my sadness and confusion and asked her how to stay connected to her while I met my needs for fun and adventure. This would have been an inclusive solution—including all my inner divine qualities as well as all the beings involved.

I'm convinced that letting go of thinking in terms of right and wrong—with its accompanying guilt, shame, and fear—is essential to our ability to grow spiritually into the higher dimensions. I certainly don't want limiting mental beliefs to keep me from that growth; therefore, I'm choosing to change my habit of judgmental thinking, and I'm willing to do the work to make it happen. It's a process, and each step along the way has its noticeable fruits and rewards.

Mary continues by addressing another common source of guilt for many people: the belief that we've caused someone else pain. She tells us that we do not cause another's pain; we're not even powerful enough to do so. That definitely gets my attention. Pain is an inherent part of the experience of duality in third-dimensional reality, and it's also part of the way beings in this dimension receive lessons to help them grow. Mary calls pain our ally and says that when we try to assume responsibility for another's pain, we're interfering with their spiritual journey.

This idea of assuming responsibility for another as interference contradicts the way many of us have been taught to think, which is to assume that if someone feels pain in response to our actions, it means we caused the pain. Then, since we caused the pain, it's our responsibility to relieve it. A corollary to this is: Whether we caused someone's pain or not, if we're good people, it's our duty to help them get out of pain. And we definitely should do that for those we love.

Taking responsibility for other people's circumstances, however, conflicts with the principle of respect for individual free will, which is honored by beings of the higher realms. In fact, assuming responsibility for another's pain wouldn't necessarily be a service to them. Mary clearly states: "If another is in pain, do not deny them their opportunity for growth and opening to light and love."

Often, our impulse to remove another's pain comes from a desire to avoid the pain *we* experience when someone we care about is in pain. In that case, we need to check in with ourselves first. We need to feel our own emotions and connect to their source in our inner divine qualities. Frequently, we're feeling sad because we long for the well-being of our loved ones. In connecting with our own desire for well-being, we can connect with our own and others' inherent well-being in God, regardless of our experience in the moment. This can be a big step forward in the midst of pain, our own or others.

Mary goes on to clarify the difference between loving others and taking responsibility for their pain:

> To love another is to allow them their pain and to love them in the midst of it. You can support them if they choose that, and if it is for your highest good, but you cannot remove their pain, nor is it your responsibility to do so. To love another is to experience their pain with them, to be fully present for their pain, and to love and open in the midst of that.

Rather than assuming it's our job to make others' pain disappear, Mary tells us to be *present* for their pain. This involves maintaining respect for their pain as part of their spiritual process. It involves staying open and heart-connected to them and ourselves, and freely choosing to what extent we want to support them—based on whether they desire support and the degree to which we're genuinely moved to do so.

Because these are such profound concepts, I want to summarize for clarity:

- We don't cause other people's pain.

- Our actions affect others, but we don't create their pain.

- Pain is part of the nature of reality in the third dimension and an ally that helps us grow spiritually.

- Loving someone doesn't mean taking responsibility for removing their pain.

- Loving someone who's in pain involves opening ourselves to their experience of pain, staying fully present to them, and loving them in the midst of it.

- We may choose to support others, if that's what they want and what serves us, but we don't take responsibility for them or their pain.

- We respect each individual as the one in charge of his or her life, including that individual's response to pain.

I want to look at this perspective in more depth, to really understand what Mary is saying. Let's begin with the idea that we don't cause other people's pain. Once again, it's important to remember that pain does not occur *because of the external circumstance*, but because the inner divine qualities aren't being fulfilled.

For example, suppose you've made an agreement with someone to meet at a certain time and that person doesn't show up on time. You might respond in a number of ways. If you're concerned for the person's safety, you might feel worried. If you have a need for people to respect your time, you might feel irritated. You might feel bored while you wait if your need is to be engaged. Or you might feel relieved if you yourself were running late and you want to be considerate of others.

If our feelings were caused by the external circumstance—the person not arriving at the agreed-upon time—then our response would be defined by that incident, and we would respond in only one way. Obviously, that's not the case. The range of possible feelings—worry, irritation, boredom, relief, and so on—is a result of which inner divine qualities are or are not fulfilled.

Because our experience is determined not by external events but by our inner divine qualities, happiness is always possible, regardless of the external circumstances. In the example of someone not showing up at the agreed-upon time, if we were to connect with the wholeness of our inner divine qualities, our worry about safety might turn into a calm trust in the divine order of events; at the same time, we might also feel compassion for the possible suffering of the other person. Our annoyance at feeling our time isn't respected could turn into tranquility in knowing that, in truth, we are always respected. Boredom might turn into awareness of things we could choose to do that are stimulating or meaningful. And our relief from having more time would probably become ease and peace.

Staying fully connected to God regardless of our external experience is a hallmark of evolved beings. You might think of a monk or nun—perhaps even the Dalai Lama or some other spiritual figure—who, because he or she is fully connected to their inner divine qualities, is able to stay fully open to the world through the faculty of feeling. People like this don't have walls around them that keep them immune from pain. They don't need them. Their strength comes from their connection to the Divine, not from avoiding life.

This is brought poignantly home by Mary's description of her response to Yeshua in the midst of his experience of pain. She didn't isolate herself from the pain; she opened herself to both his pain and her own:

> This is what I did with Yeshua. I could not remove his pain, nor was it my responsibility to do so. He chose his spiritual path, and mine was to love him and be fully present, heart wide-open to him in his glory and his pain. This is part of the journey of light and love in this dimension.

I'm deeply grateful to Mary for sharing this most painful and deeply intimate aspect of her love relationship with Yeshua. The experience she relates in these few sentences is profoundly simple, portraying such a clear vision of what she calls us to.

Mary's final paragraphs touch me deeply because of the compassion she expresses for all of us in the third dimension. She acknowledges the inherent difficulty of this realm because it includes pain and because opening up to light and love in the third dimension also means opening to pain. However, at some point, we'll transcend our need for pain as a support for our growth. I believe this will correspond with our movement into the higher fourth dimension and beyond. In the meantime, whether we're experiencing pain or not, our spiritual response and practice are always the same: to open to love and light. This, Mary says, "is the only path that truly satisfies."

I close with Mary's words because they continually restore me to light and love:

> My message to you is simple and always the same: Stay true to light and love. Open yourself fully to light and love. Let light and love be your guide. You will know you are doing this by

your peace, by your openheartedness, by your radiance. And as you do that more and more, we will always be with you, supporting you on your path home to light and love....We welcome you, dear ones, with joy and anticipation.

TWENTY-ONE

From Blame to Love

Greetings, my dear one ~

You have come far on your path of love. You are understanding how to communicate love through your words, which is so important in this dimension. Your words are powerful instruments of manifestation. Through your words, energy is carried and creates form. Many people have the idea that words are not significant, but this is not so. It was understood in more ancient times that words carry power. Words can be the carriers of prayer. Indeed, all words, and truly all thoughts, are a form of prayer. Whatever you think, and even more so, whatever you say, is a kind of invocation. It can bring positive or negative energy. It is up to you. You are cocreators in this realm, though often your creations don't manifest immediately, so you don't tend to be aware that what is happening to you is something that you actually manifested. Many of you believe that things are happening to you from outside forces, because of other people or other events. What you don't realize is that your own energy, carried through thoughts and words, has brought these people and actions into your life.

It always comes back to you. And this is where your great power is, with yourself. If you want to affect what is happening in your life and world, change yourself. Change your thoughts and your words specifically. And the first way that this change happens is to stop thinking that others are responsible for the way you're feeling. Stop blaming others, through your thoughts and words, for your experience. You may be affected by others because you are not immune. Accept the relationship, the effect. That is not blame. That is opening to relationship.

That noticing of relationship crosses over into blame if you add judgment to it. If there is any degree of judgment in your thinking or speech that someone did anything wrong or bad, then you have crossed over into blame. This is actually a crucial spiritual distinction and awareness to hold, because once you are in the mind-set of blame, all your attention and energy is going to the other and you have emptied yourself of your power, your light, your love. Do not do that. It is not necessary, and it does not serve you.

This distinction is so important and is very difficult for so many of you to see because you have been trained to blame in your culture, trained to put all of your focus and energy and attention on others and what they did wrong or bad. You've been trained to think that someone is at fault, and your job is to figure out who it is. And you work very hard to try to find someone other than yourself who is at fault because you assume that the one who is at fault will lose their connection to love, that they don't deserve love because they have been bad or wrong.

It doesn't help you at all to make others wrong. As children, if your parents or caretakers made you wrong, by criticizing you and telling you that you were bad, you learned to associate being wrong or bad with losing love, and being right or good with receiving love. Then life became a game of proving that you were right or others were wrong in order to be loved. This kind of training is very damaging because receiving love has nothing to do with being right or avoiding being wrong. Ironically, the whole game of right and wrong is a huge obstacle to receiving love or to being love. If you have learned that game, as so many of you have, you must now undo that thinking within yourself. Be willing to let go of striving to be right or proving that others are wrong. Stand vulnerable and open-hearted in your experience, including your pain, and discover whether you are loved.

God never abandons anyone. You simply turn away from God by closing your hearts and going into your minds. Let go of your thinking-barricade that others or yourself have done something wrong, and stand vulnerable in your heart. See what you experience. See if God exists and if God loves you.

I have no doubt of the outcome of that experiment. I have no doubt of God or God's love. But do not take my word for it. Find out for yourself. Set your defenses aside and see if God is there for you, waiting to love you and shine the Creator-Light through you. I joyfully await the results of your discovery.

I love you most profoundly and send you my blessings.
I AM Mary Magdalene

*M*ary begins this communication by telling us that our words are powerful instruments of manifestation. Whether we recognize it or not, our speech and thoughts are forms of prayer through which we create our reality. But because our manifestations don't necessarily appear immediately, we may not notice the relationship between what we think and communicate and our ensuing reality.

In third-dimensional consciousness, we tend to believe things happen to us from the outside, due to external forces beyond our control. This is the foundation of what could be called victim consciousness: "It's not my fault," "I had to," "I didn't have a choice," "They or that thing made me do it." In the fourth dimension and above, we begin to understand that we are the creators of our reality and whatever appears in our lives is a result of what we've called in.

This is actually good news, although if we're committed to victim consciousness, we may not view it that way. We may interpret the idea that we create our own reality as meaning we're to blame for any experiences we don't enjoy. But blaming ourselves is just as much of a waste of energy as blaming someone else, and it's a block to claiming our power. If we accept that we create our lives—not to judge ourselves but simply to be in right relationship to reality—we then become empowered creators, and we can intelligently discern whether what we create is serving us. If it's not, we can change it. What a gift!

In creating our reality, we're still affected by other beings and forms of life, all of which are also part of our creation. This is because we're connected to all others, so we all affect each other. However, noticing that something has affected us is different from blame. It's not until we add judgments and make someone at fault that blame arises. For example, if your partner expresses political views at a family gathering that challenge those of your family, the effect might be to stimulate discomfort or disagreement. You can just observe what is happening without judging the situation. This is different from blaming your partner for wrecking the evening, being insensitive to others, not being able to just relax and have fun, or other variations in a similar vein.

This distinction between judgment and observation of cause and effect isn't easy for most of us because we're so used to blaming and hearing others' blame. It takes a lot of awareness and intention to break out of this habit. The first step is to notice that we have a choice: we can make others wrong or at fault, or we can choose to simply notice what occurred and its effect.

As we become stronger in taking full responsibility for all the events in our lives, we'll find that outer occurrences have increasingly less power to disconnect us from God. We become more stable and rested in joy, peace, and harmony. This stability arises not because we've built a barrier between us and the world, or denied that we're affected by the world; rather it's because we've become connected to our inner divine qualities—and through those, to God—so that we can be fully in the world but not of it.

Mary suggests that, as children, many of us learned to blame others and deny our own responsibility so that our parents or caretakers would love us. We assumed we'd only be loved if we could prove that we were right and someone else was at fault. She points out the sad irony in this because "the whole game of right and wrong is a huge obstacle to receiving love or to being love." She continues:

> If you have learned that game, as so many of you have, you must now undo that thinking within yourself. Be willing to let go of striving to be right or proving that others are wrong. Stand vulnerable and openhearted in your experience, including your pain, and discover whether you are loved.

Mary's words speak to the core in all of us, to the place where we all long to love and to be loved. For me, her description of opening our hearts in vulnerability calls forth an image of a young, tender child receiving love with open arms. Once again, Mary helps us to find our way, so that we may experience the fulfillment of our deepest desires.

Mary closes on the same note, challenging us to see what happens when we let go of right-wrong thinking and blame. She asks us to notice, once we cease to blame others or think in terms of right and wrong, if God exists and if God loves us. Does God withhold love from us, as perhaps we experienced our parents doing when we didn't conform to their desires? Or are we choosing to avoid feelings and so close ourselves from God's love? When we open to our feelings, do we experience God and love? She urges us to find out, even as she reveals her reality and truth:

> I have no doubt of the outcome of that experiment. I have no doubt of God or God's love. But do not take my word for it. Find out for yourself. Set your defenses aside and see if God is there for you, waiting to love you and shine the Creator-Light through you. I joyfully await the results of your discovery.

TWENTY-TWO

Evolving into Unconditional Love

Greetings, beloved ~

You are coming to understand why I speak so much about the importance of feeling and, in particular, feeling pain. I will explain more about this. Many of you have the sense that unconditional love is an important aspect of evolving into your highest self, and this is correct. However, for most of you, it is still just an idea, and you don't understand how to achieve this.

This is because unconditional love is rooted in the Second Ray of the Divine, which is the ray of the Divine Feminine. Up until now, the ray that has been dominant on Earth is the First Ray of divine will, which is the ray of the Divine Masculine. This is why so much of your spiritual teachings, up until this point, have focused on things like clearing the mind of false beliefs and opening to higher consciousness, activating the will to do God's work in the world, and manifesting a higher reality in this dimension.

Now, at this time in the evolution of Earth and for all of you who are incarnate here, there is an influx of new divine energies, which is creating a shift and a grand opportunity for accelerated growth and transformation. These new energies are here because you are now receiving the Second Ray of the Divine Feminine. Yet, in order to fully receive this, you must be open at the level of feeling.

Your heart is the organ of reception and activation of this energy, and it is through your ability to feel that this energy is carried.

So feeling is essential to receiving and activating this new energy. Your job at this time is to open fully as feeling beings. You are being called to love yourself unconditionally, with no conditions or limits upon that self-love. And in the domain of feeling, this is especially about loving all of your emotions. They all have a divine purpose. Do you think you would be given the magnificent range of feelings and emotions that you all possess for no purpose? Do you think this was a kind of design error? No, dear ones, your feelings are to serve you, and they are a great help to you if you understand this and are in the correct relationship to them. Your feelings are a tremendous asset and a unique gift that you in this realm have been given. Yet, as I have said before, many have planted the idea that emotions are bad or harmful and should be denied, suppressed, disengaged from. This is actually the opposite of the truth.

As you learn to love your emotions, including all of the painful ones, you will be practicing the foundation of unconditional love. In this loving, you will open to your feelings; you will feel them, which is different from reacting to them. In your reaction, you either try to avoid them, make them go away, or act upon them. But feeling is none of these things. Feeling is simply being with the feelings, embracing them and merging with them, so that they can give you their gifts. Feelings are the messengers of your divine attributes that live within you. They will lead you to these beautiful qualities within that are your bridge to God. This is the way of the open heart, the Divine Feminine path of unconditional love. And it is the path you are called to walk and embrace and radiate from in your open heart. It is a glorious song of love.

And there is another energy that is shining upon Earth at this time, and it is the Third Ray of divine wisdom. In this ray, the First and Second Rays of divine will and divine love experience the union of their qualities as divine wisdom. This is one of the forms of the Trinity as it manifests in your realm. The First Ray carries the qualities of the Divine Father, the Second Ray carries the qualities of the Divine Mother, and the Third Ray carries the qualities of the union of the Divine Father and Mother, giving birth to the Divine Child. This Divine Child can also be seen as your I AM presence.

You are living in a most wondrous time, when so many aspects of the Divine are being revealed to you so abundantly and openly. In the past, very few had access to these divine rays, only those who had purified themselves to an extraordinary degree. But now it is different. The divine powers are being showered down upon you so freely, yet you must do your part to receive them. If you are in the midst of the mightiest rain but hold an umbrella over your head, you will not receive any of the water flowing around you.

And so you must do your part to open up and receive this divine downpour. And one of the primary arenas for most of you is at the level of feeling. This is your bridge to unconditional love, and it begins with unconditional love of yourself, all of who you are, and especially of your emotions and feelings. It begins with opening at the heart to your feelings, reversing your patterns of closing yourself off from your emotions and feelings. Open to them and let them guide you to your higher self. And as you learn to love your feelings unconditionally, you will naturally become a conduit of unconditional love. It is inevitable.

I wish to give an example because I know that this is a confusing arena for many of you, due to all the misinformation you have received about emotions. Let's say that someone has said something to you that is painful for you to hear, something such as, "That's so selfish of you. You're always only thinking of yourself!" You might have an immediate reaction come up. For example, you might want to lash out at them with a criticism of them, which is a way of fighting back, proving that they're wrong so their judgment of you isn't valid. This could happen verbally or just in your thoughts. Another reaction you might have is to want to defend yourself, proving how their accusation isn't true. Or you might want to take an action, wanting to hurt them physically or to withdraw from them in some way.

All of these are reactions to the pain you feel from the comment, ways of trying to make the pain go away. Instead of all of these reactions, you could simply feel the pain. You could open to it, experience it. Breathe into it, relax into it, open yourself to it. And with this, you could ask yourself, "What is the source of this pain within me?" The source will be different each time, a different quality or divine attribute that you carry within. In this example, the source may be that you're wanting acceptance and to be understood for your actual intentions and motives. Acceptance and understanding are two of the entire range of beautiful divine attributes that live within you. As you open to the experience of your hurt, you can let that lead you to your longing for acceptance and understanding. And when you connect with those inner divine attributes, you will experience a shift. You will be crossing over the bridge to your connection with God.

What is so wonderful is that you can always do this, at any time or in any circumstance, because these qualities are always within you; truly they *are* you. You are incredibly powerful, and you always have the ability to connect with God. Nothing can ever stand in the way of this because this is who and what you are.

Your feelings are one of your greatest allies—they are always guiding you to this awakening to God. Now, at this time in your evolution, you are being called to embrace your feelings as your pathway to unconditional love. I support you in this most fully, as I know this path profoundly as a true and wondrous path to God.

I love you and bless you with all my heart
in your continued unfoldment.
I AM Mary Magdalene

*A*s I received this message from Mary, I sensed she was starting to wind down her communications and was almost finished with what she wanted to say. I saw this message as the final recapitulation of her most important material: her instruction about opening to feeling as the platform for moving into unconditional love.

I felt sad as I anticipated the end of her daily, intimate communications. During the entire time I had been receiving her messages, she consistently drew me into her state and perspective, and through her spiritual transmission, I experienced my inherent state of union with God. It was a gift too enormous to ever comprehend with my mind, and I felt such gratitude for all that I'd received and experienced. I also felt tremendous responsibility for the wealth of instruction and guidance I'd been entrusted with. By this time, I was well aware of Mary's strong intention that this body of teaching should reach as many people as possible, as quickly as possible—and that she was counting on me to make that happen.

I sensed her subtly helping me to transition from the relatively passive role of recipient of her messages to the active role of communicator so that I could make her messages accessible to people everywhere. Even though I felt sad about letting go of our meetings, I also trusted her wisdom and guidance in this whole process, which included trusting that I would be able to do what she was asking of me. While I guessed that this might be her last message, I valued it all the more as I once again received her words and clarion call.

Mary begins by asserting the importance of unconditional love as an essential step in our spiritual growth, adding that, for most of us, this kind of love is still just a concept we don't know how to achieve. She explains that unconditional love is rooted in the Second Ray of the Divine, the ray of the Divine Feminine, which carries the energy of divine love. Up until now, this ray hasn't been generally accessible, which is why unconditional love has been so difficult for us.

In the past, we have primarily experienced the First Ray of divine will—the energy of the Divine Masculine. The Divine Masculine is characterized by will and intention, which consciously direct and engage our minds, bodies, and personal power to achieve desired goals. Thus, much of our spirituality has been focused on disciplining our beliefs, thinking, and actions, and, on that basis, achieving desired outcomes.

Now, however, several new divine energies have been activated in our world. The initial one, the Second Ray of divine love, requires us to be open at the level of feeling because feeling is the medium that allows our heart to receive and activate this divine energy within ourselves. Mary tells us that our job at this time is to open fully as feeling beings, which will allow us to grow into unconditional love. I greatly appreciate the clarity and simplicity of this job description. It conjures up an image of total openness with a natural kind of strength. We are strong because, in our openness, everything moves through us without any resistance.

Mary then describes the progression of growing into unconditional love. The first step is to love *ourselves* unconditionally, which specifically involves loving all of our emotions. When most of us contemplate the concept of unconditional love, we generally imagine ourselves loving others unconditionally. To think about loving ourselves unconditionally, especially as our first step, is fairly unusual. But to think about loving our emotions unconditionally is downright rare. Still, when I look at the progression logically, this line of reasoning makes perfect sense. Most people agree that if we want to manifest something in our outer reality, we must first realize it within ourselves. Therefore, if we want to love others unconditionally, we must start with loving ourselves unconditionally. And, of course, unconditional love of self would include *all* parts of us.

One essential part of ourselves that many of us have rejected, denied, and failed to love is our emotional aspect, especially our painful emotions. We feel we need to escape our emotions and that it would be better if we didn't even have them. Mary addresses our attitude toward our emotions when she asks us, "Do you think you would be given the magnificent range of feelings and emotions that you all possess for no purpose? Do you think this was a kind of design error?"

I love these questions! I see them illuminating a subtle belief that our emotions are not an essential, or even supportive, part of our being—that they're a kind of random, extraneous phenomena that doesn't actually serve us and we'd be better off without. We could easily conclude that it's best to detach ourselves as much as possible from our feelings, like separating the wheat from the chaff. But Mary's questions imply that in doubting and discounting our emotions, we actually doubt and discount God.

Mary then answers her own questions about the purpose of emotions with great sincerity and gentleness:

> No, dear ones, your feelings are to serve you, and they are a great help to you if you understand this and are in the correct relationship to them. Your feelings are a tremendous asset and a unique gift that you in this realm have been given. Yet, as I

have said before, many have planted the idea that emotions are bad or harmful and should be denied, suppressed, disengaged from. This is actually the opposite of the truth.

Having once again emphasized the value of our feelings, Mary returns to the theme of loving all our emotions, especially the painful ones, through allowing ourselves to fully feel them. This begins the process of letting our feelings take us to Source. Since this process has been described earlier, I will summarize it here:

1. Fully feel your emotions. Embrace them and merge with them.

2. Allow your feelings to lead you to their source, which will always be one or more of your inner divine qualities. (For help identifying these, see the list in figure 2-1.) You may use your mind to guide you in determining which specific qualities are the source of your feelings.

3. Once you've identified the particular inner divine qualities that are the source of your feelings, connect with your longing for those qualities in your situation or your celebration of their fulfillment. Give yourself as much time as you need for this process, accepting all the feelings that arise.

4. Experience the shift into your inherent and ongoing connection with those inner divine qualities in their fullness.

5. Take time and space to be with the peace of your reconnection with God, integrating any new changes or understandings you receive. Wait to act until you feel the energy of movement naturally arising.

6. Let your actions come from your connection to God. These actions will have a different feeling-quality than actions you may have taken initially to get out of the pain. You will feel whole and peaceful at your core, and you will have clarity about how to proceed. Often, unexpected solutions will come

to you because your creativity has opened up, fueled by the integration of all the parts of yourself with the Divine.

The example Mary used to demonstrate these steps came from an actual incident in my life. Someone called me selfish and said I always thought only about myself. After this person's remark, I felt both hurt and frustrated: I was hurt because I wanted acceptance and frustrated because I wanted to be understood as I truly was in the situation—as opposed to what the other person had assumed about me. In this situation, my inner divine qualities of acceptance and understanding weren't being fulfilled.

A shift occurred when I was able to connect with those qualities of acceptance and understanding within myself, and I was able to feel and experience how they live within me, independent of anything in the external world. In doing so, I once again felt sustained, full, and peaceful. In that reconnection, all my doors to the Divine once again opened, and I felt a sense of being held in God. That state of union with God reminds me of the term *divine order*, because I felt a sense of rightness or order in my world. I was realigned to the Divine, and all was well.

This process of engaging our feelings and letting them take us to God constitutes what Mary calls "the Divine Feminine path of unconditional love." She says we're called to walk and embrace and radiate this path from our open hearts, and she portrays this as "a glorious song of love." I notice her description differs from the common notion of unconditional love as an almost warrior-like path of loving, marked by challenge. Mary's path of unconditional love is a path of surrender: we surrender to our feelings, and through that surrender we open to God, to our hearts, and to love.

Mary goes on to speak about the other divine ray being activated at this time: the Third Ray of divine wisdom in action. This ray is also known as the Divine Child, and it's associated with our I AM presence, which is the presence of God in its individualized form within each of us. The Third Ray could be described as "I AM the Divine Child of the Divine Masculine and Feminine in union with each other."

Mary points out that the relationship of all three rays to each other forms a trinity—a primary and universal form of the trinity that's clearly different from the trinity described in many religions. In contrast to the Father-Son-Holy Spirit in Christianity, or Brahma-Vishnu-Shiva in Hinduism, or maiden-mother-crone in the Pagan/Wiccan tradition, the trinity of the first three God rays is completely balanced between the Masculine and the Feminine. And it includes all creation as God.

One expression of this trinity is that our Father God and Mother God produce the Divine Child as all of us. In this perspective, Yeshua is *not* the only son of a Masculine God but the child of a God who is both Masculine and Feminine. And while Yeshua is a Divine Child, so are we all. I hear him allude to our shared divinity in the biblical passage in which he says, "This and more shall you do."

Another form of the trinity offers us a more human model and template. In this trinity, I see Yeshua representing the Divine Masculine, Mary Magdalene representing the Divine Feminine, and their Sacred Union producing the Divine Child. Perhaps literal biological children were produced from their union, but I interpret the Divine Child in a much broader sense. I see them supporting the birth of us all into our divine selves in our ascended, fifth-dimensional form.

Mary explains that we're living in a remarkable time when divine powers are showering down upon us. In the past, access to these higher energies needed to be earned through challenging processes of spiritual development, but today we are bountifully and generously given access to them. Nevertheless, we must still do our part to receive all the available blessings and support. A key aspect of our part is to open to our feelings; if we don't do this, we're like people holding up umbrellas in the midst of a downpour. The stream of these divine rays can rain freely upon us, but if we're not open through our channel of feeling, we won't receive this divine offering.

When we open our hearts through our feelings, Mary assures us we'll be guided to our higher self and we'll become a conduit for unconditional love. In fact, she's so confident about this process that she says opening to our feelings will *definitely* lead us into living as unconditional love. While this process isn't necessarily easy—primarily because we're so deeply conditioned to shut down our feelings—I, nonetheless, feel greatly encouraged by her declaration.

Mary continues, "You are incredibly powerful, and you always have the ability to connect with God. Nothing can ever stand in the way of this because this is who and what you are." Again, I value her absolute trust in this process, along with her complete trust in our ability to do what she recommends.

Mary closes this message with the bold statement that our feelings are one of our *greatest allies* in guiding us to awakening in God. She affirms once more that we are to embrace our feelings as the pathway to unconditional love. And she tells us that she profoundly knows this path as a true and wondrous path to God.

It is this last sentence that touches me most deeply. I am reminded of what Mary herself went through and the emotions she must have felt as she witnessed her lover, life partner, teacher, and the one she knew as God in human form being mocked, tortured, and brutally killed; as she lived with so many people's hatred and misrepresentation of her as a woman; as she watched Yeshua's followers being persecuted and murdered; and as she saw Yeshua's teaching maligned, suppressed, altered, and obscured. In light of all she experienced and felt in her relationship with Yeshua, for her to tell us the path of feeling is not only a true, but a *wondrous* path to God affects me profoundly. I hear her telling us that this path has led her to where she is now, full of light and love and wisdom, in union with God. I trust what she has learned and understood through all she has gone through. I trust the sincerity of her desire to help us. And I trust that this path has gifts and help for a great many of us.

I give deepest thanks to Mary for sharing all her wisdom, including the path of opening to feeling, so directly and forthrightly.

PART VI

Mary Shares of Herself

TWENTY-THREE

My Love for Yeshua

Greetings again, my beloved ~

Today, I wish to talk to you about love. This is such a tender topic; it is not easy to put into words. So I shall tell you about my love for Yeshua.

There is a place in my heart where Yeshua lives. I prize this place, and it is holy beyond words. It is so holy, so full of love, it is almost painful. The physical heart, even the physical being, can barely receive and shelter this kind of love. It is so deep, so profound, so all-encompassing. It is personal and it also goes beyond the personal. I cannot tell the difference between my love of God and my love of Yeshua. My love of Yeshua opens me to God.

I have not done this. It is a pure gift from God. It is God's way of loving me and drawing me to the Divine. And every moment of love is the same, regardless of the person who stimulates that love or even the circumstance. You might feel profound love when you see a gorgeous sunset, an exquisite landscape, or a beautiful flower. These, too, are God reaching out to your heart. And always the response is to open to love. That is all that is required. Open to love, and you will be guided by love.

Love is not a choice between you and someone else, where you choose them over you. Love is a merging at the heart, where you open and join the other in union. It is a oneness, and out of that one-ness you are moved.

The more you experience that oneness in life, the more you will act from love, will *be* love. That is where you are all headed, and it is ecstasy.

I invoke that all may know the beauty of love as I have known it with Yeshua. It will break your heart open to God, and you will receive all the riches of the universe.

So be it, and so it is.
In love, I AM Mary Magdalene

*T*his was the sweetest message I received from Mary. In her previous communications, I felt her bringing a palpable sense of urgency and a laser-like focus to the topics. Now it seemed she had said all she wanted to say and could finally relax. She spoke more peacefully and quietly, as though she were gently lifting the veil of her life in friend-ship and trust to give us a glimpse of her intimate relationship with Yeshua. She did this not because she wants to tell us about the de-tails of their life together, but because she wants to guide us toward what she knows about pure love.

Every time I read this message, I am returned to a deep experience of openhearted, undefended love. I feel the exquisiteness of which she speaks: my heart knows it, my skin tingles with it, and my being longs for it.

I have very little to say about this message. I suspect that my words would only detract from Mary's perfect expression. My only thought is an echo of Mary's invocation: May we all know the beauty of love as Mary has known it with Yeshua. May it break our hearts wide-open to God.

After receiving this message, I wondered if it was the final one, a closure of my time with Mary. As it turned out, there would be two more.

TWENTY-FOUR

Opening to God through Sexuality

I AM here, dear one,
and I bring you more messages of light and love ~

I am now ready to speak to you of sexuality. I have waited to talk
about this because there is much confusion in this area. That is
largely because you have work to do to open yourselves up at the
level of feeling and, on that basis, to be open to love. This is why I
began by speaking about feeling and love, because they are the foundation for relating to another, especially intimately.

It is possible to be sexual with oneself, and this is not a sin as
some would have you believe. There is nothing bad or wrong or
evil or dirty with sexuality in any way, any more than there is something dirty or bad or evil or wrong with eating food. Both are bodily
functions that support your life here, and both can be related to as
forms of communion with the Divine.

When you take food, you begin with prayer, offering thanks and
gratitude for what you're receiving. The disposition of gratitude is a
form of prayer that aligns you to your higher self and opens you to
God. It is one of the simplest and most direct forms of communion.
Always begin your prayers with gratitude, with aligning yourself to
all the ways you are receiving the Divine in this moment.

To continue with the analogy of food taking, through offering prayer and strengthening your disposition of gratitude, you call in the energy of blessing and communion. You are blessing and thanking all the elements, all the life that has gone into the food and which is now feeding you, granting you life, and supporting and sustaining the life in you. You have merged with the energy of life that is coming from the food, through gratitude and blessing. This transforms the food, and it also transforms you. Through opening your heart in love and gratitude to the food, you are activating the pure light that is available to you through the process of taking in food. The food will taste better, more alive and delicious, when you are in this disposition. And it actually is, because you are receiving more than just food. You are communing with the Creator through your food taking.

The process of sexuality is also a form of communion with the Creator. Your prayer is your open, feeling heart, which opens you to love. To engage this kind of communion, you must be strong in knowing how to feel. And you must know how to make this feeling connection with your partner. If there is pain in your heart, even something that you consider small or insignificant, you must open to it and share it with your partner. Learn to share your pain and your joy together, not to fix it or to figure it out, but to let your hearts merge at the feeling level. As you have learned to open to your own pain and let that take you to God, in partnership, you must be able to open to your partner's pain and let that take you to God together.

This is the container for sexuality, that your hearts are merged. Then your bodies can open in God, and your loving will transform you, will strengthen your reception of God's light. If you do not do this, your sexuality will empty you, and you will crave for what you did not receive. Know that it is not in the other. It is in your heart opening to God. That is the source that feeds and fills and fulfills you. And to find this in sexuality, you must know how to open your heart to God with your partner.

Sexuality is also a powerful medium for moving you into the higher dimensions. There are techniques that support this that have been passed down through the ages in some of your teachings, such as Tantra. But these techniques will not serve their purpose if you have not first learned to open to feeling and love, with yourself and with your partner. Sexuality becomes communion when it is founded on love and activated by your loving heart and the union of your heart with your partner.

Many of you have shame about your sexuality and about your bodies. This has been instilled in you to control you, often unknowingly, by those who had the same thing instilled in them. It is another means of keeping you from your power, because sexuality is a powerful force.

Your bodies are beautiful and divine in all their forms. Do not neglect them. You should care for them lovingly, including eating foods that serve the light and life in you and getting enough movement and exercise so that your body is strong and pleasurably open to receiving and transmitting light and life. You should adorn your body as a temple of God, for truly that is what it is. But don't mistake the temple for the light and love of God.

Enjoy your body and others' bodies like pieces of beautiful art in infinite forms of manifestation that communicate the beauty of God. There is not just one look or one shape that is beautiful or perfect, and everything else is lacking or somehow deficient. All temples shine with the beauty of God if you know how to see that. It is especially apparent in children because their light is still bright, not dimmed by concepts of shame and burdened by the darkness of the mind. You are not meant to lose that as you age. Truly, that light would become more refined and focused if you weren't carrying the shields of your mind and your ideas of wrongness that lead you to feelings such as shame and guilt and depression and most of your anger. Those aren't natural feelings, because they're infused with ideas of wrongness.

Many of you must learn to love your bodies again, because you have become divorced from them with your ideas of wrongness and badness and not-good-enoughness. Imagine your body as a beautiful child, and think of how you would want to love that child and to have that child receive love. You also need to guide the child to things that will support the child's life and light and love. And so it is with your body. Love is not the same as indulgence. Indulgence is something you do when you're lacking love and seeking a compensation for that lack, yet it never works. Only love fulfills you.

When you love your own body, then you can open to love with another through the physical. And your love transforms that process into a beautiful sharing and opening to your greater self, which includes your physical, includes your feeling, includes your sexual energy. Your mind becomes open and is in service to your feeling being, which is the right relationship of the mind to your other functions. And you are available to be carried in love to God.

Sexuality is a doorway that opens you to union with God. For most people, sexual experiences are relatively brief, but you can learn to expand this doorway through techniques such as Tantra. This is valuable as a support for transforming your physical body, your emotional body, your mental body, and your energy body. In awakened sexuality, you are aligning these bodies and unifying them to open to the Divine. This is a valuable practice when it is engaged in this way, with this understanding. You engage this with a partner, although it can also be engaged with yourself. When you are engaging sexuality with your partner, it is profoundly bonding because of the depth you are opening yourself to and the power of the divine communion you are connecting with. It is a wondrous and beautiful sacrament to engage this with another, one of the great gifts of this realm.

I love you dearly and am here to support you in your opening to God.
I AM Mary Magdalene

I see this message as a finishing stroke—a way of placing the last piece in a puzzle or completing a circle and returning to the starting point. In her early messages, Mary talked about our bodies, sexuality, and emotions as primary aspects of the Divine Feminine. She went on, in subsequent communications, to discuss the need to relate to our emotions and let them lead us to God. By contrast, she said very little about how we relate to our bodies, other than emphasizing the importance of healing any shame about them. I think she knows we have access to ample information about how to love and heal our bodies, so she was content for us to understand that loving our bodies is one of the basic ways the Divine Feminine manifests in our reality.

Mary wove the discussion of sexuality throughout her first six messages, ending with the description of her sacred relationship with Yeshua, which included sacred sexuality as part of their spiritual path of transformation. She then turned her attention to other topics—and intentionally left sexuality out of the discussion—focusing on our need to open up to our feelings and to love as the foundation for both the awakened heart and intimate relationships. Now, after finishing the discussion about opening to our feelings and love, she is finally ready to return to the topic of sexuality.

She begins by stating that there's nothing sinful about sexuality, including being sexual with oneself. Sexuality is like eating food, in that both eating and sex are natural bodily functions that support life, and both can be used as a form of communion with the Divine.

Before we eat, Mary tells us to begin with prayers and gratitude because these align us to our higher self and open us to receiving from God. With gratitude, we bless our food and invite in the life force carried in the food. This sacred act of prayer transforms both us and the food, activating the pure light energy of the food and turning the act of eating into divine communion.

Sexuality can also be a form of communion with the Creator. In sexuality, however, our prayer isn't necessarily a verbal communication; it's our open, feeling heart engaged in love with our partner. This view of prayer differs from the more traditional understanding of prayer as a verbal expression of intention and will. Prayer as a movement of love from the heart, engaged with a partner, seems like a beautiful Feminine form of prayer—just as sexuality is a manifestation of the Divine Feminine, for both men and women.

Engaging in sexuality as a prayer of love requires us to be strong and open to feelings, and to be able to share emotions with our partner. Mary instructs us to share both our pain and our joy with our partner, not with the intention of fixing the other but in order to merge our hearts through feeling. First, we allowed our individual pain to take us to God; now we allow our partner's pain and joy to take us to God—together.

When we're able to merge hearts with our partner, then we're ready to merge our bodies. If we ignore our heart connection, our sexuality will be empty and we'll remain unsatisfied. We won't have received what we're really seeking and what really satisfies us, which is union with the Divine.

Mary affirms the power of sexuality to transform us and move us into the higher dimensions when we open to God in this way. This may be one of the reasons we humans are so drawn to sexuality—sex is one of the most accessible ways to taste the bliss and freedom of the higher dimensions. We can learn techniques through practices such as Tantra to support our transformation through sexuality, but these still require a foundation of feeling and love to serve their purpose. *The communion of sexuality must be activated by our loving hearts and heart union with our partner.*

Because sexuality is such a powerful force, shame about our sexuality and our bodies is used as a method to control it. Shame inhibits our sexual expression so that we don't become too free in God's ecstasy, but rather channel our life force according to the dictates of authority. Usually, people aren't even conscious of using shame to manipulate others; they are simply passing on what was instilled in them. However, Mary says our bodies aren't shameful; they're beautiful vessels of God, temples for divine communion. She urges us to care for them in all ways, yet not be fooled into worshiping the temple itself. As she puts it, "Don't mistake the temple for the light and love of God."

I value this clarification. Mary tells us to love our bodies fully: Love them through all their changes, serve them well and faithfully, relate to them as manifestations of God, and commune with God through them; but don't become a devotee of the body or of sexuality. As with all else, we can let our bodies and our sexuality take us to God.

One way of communing with God is to enjoy both our own and others' bodies; we can appreciate the form of our bodies in the same way we enjoy beautiful artwork. Enjoy all the different shapes and forms, for they all, in their own way, communicate the beauty of God. Contemporary media and culture generally promote one particular human shape and form as beautiful: a youthful, slender woman and a youthful, muscular man. Mary calls us to move beyond our conditioning about physical appearance to see the beauty in all forms. Then we can receive and enjoy God's light as it manifests in and as all of us.

We often find it easier to see the divinity in children because they still shine their light clearly and openly. But our light dims with age as ideas of good/bad and right/wrong lock in feelings of shame, guilt, depression, and anger. (Mary calls all of these "unnatural feelings" because they're fed by ideas of wrongness.) The result is that we block our God-Light and mute our experience of God.

How do we change this? We begin with ourselves, by learning to love our bodies again. Mary suggests that we imagine our bodies as beautiful children we want to love. We can see the beauty of our bodies, and we can learn to enjoy them and care for them just as we would care for a beloved child. Of course, care is not the same as indulgence; indulgence is what we do when we're lacking love.

While I was following a raw foods diet based on a teaching called Instinctive Eating, I began to understand how loving, enjoying, and caring for our bodies differs from indulgence. In the Instinctive Eating approach, sensory information—smell, taste, and visual appearance—is used to determine what foods the body needs. Foods in their raw, unadulterated state are attractive and pleasurable to us if our body needs them. If our body doesn't need them, we're not attracted to them. Thus, we choose what to eat based on our body's sensory feedback.

This explains the function of sensual attraction. It's a mechanism that guides us to what we need for our sustenance. A good example is how animals in the wild select their food: they use their senses of sight, smell, and taste and then respond on the basis of what they're attracted to.

I became completely healthy through following Instinctive Eating, and I did it by following the pleasure of my senses rather than my ideas about what I should be eating. I also enjoyed the taste of my food more than I ever had, and I was guided to stop eating when the pleasure waned. Most profoundly, I learned to trust my body and my experience of pleasure as something that supported me. This approach differs sharply from the common cultural attitude that following pleasure leads to trouble, so we need to control ourselves to stay safe from the dangers and temptations of pleasure. Rather than trying to clamp down on our desire for pleasure, we need to become aligned to the true function of pleasure, which is to support us.

Once we're rightly aligned to pleasure and have learned to love our own bodies, we're able to open to love with another person. We open all of us, including our physical bodies, sexual energy, feelings, and minds; we open to our partner and our higher self. Then, Mary tells us, we're "available to be carried in love to God." That sounds wonderful to me.

In the final portion of this message, Mary gives an overview of the possibilities for sexuality as a doorway to union with God. While most people engage in sexuality as a relatively brief experience, she says we can learn to expand this doorway through techniques such as Tantra. In awakened sexuality, we create a deep bond with our partner because of the depth of our opening and the shared communion with God. Sexuality becomes an integral part of our communion with the Divine and a potent form of transformation in God. Mary closes this message by affirming that awakened sexuality is "a wondrous and beautiful sacrament to engage…with another, one of the great gifts of this realm."

As in the previous communication, Mary had a calm and rested quality as she gave me this message. I sensed she had finished her "how to" of particular practices. This message functioned to fill out her picture of sexuality and show it as part of the total life she's calling us to, a life of union with the Divine Masculine and Feminine. I believe she has much more to say about awakened sexuality and will share that at a future time. For now, I sense her completion with this topic.

PART VII

The Call to All Hearts

TWENTY-FIVE

Join the River of Love

Beloved ones ~

I come again to talk with you about the heart. All I have said to you can be summarized as this: Open your heart, feel from your heart, live from your heart. Let your mind be in service to your heart. It really is that simple, but for most of you, it is not easy. That is why I have talked so much about what you must do to be able to do this. More than anything, it is about regaining your capacity for feeling. This capacity has been intentionally shut down in you to make you easy to control. Even as very young children, most of you received messages that told you feelings were bad or forbidden if you wanted to be loved and accepted. Often you received these messages from parents who actually loved you and meant to support you, but they were just passing on the messages and training they'd received.

Have you ever wondered why your school system is almost exclusively geared toward training your mind and most of you have received virtually no instruction in feeling or in how to use your emotions? This is not an oversight or an accident. It is done intentionally to produce productive members of society who are obedient and submissive and who will devote their life energy to doing what they are told without following their own impulses and desires. I realize that it may be very difficult to see yourselves this way, very painful, and may also bring up mourning for what you have lost in the process.

Do you remember a young child, yourself, who had dreams and fantasies and passions, who believed in yourself and your desires? That child part of you usually gets trained out in your education system, a place where you become trained to do what's right and work for rewards, which teaches you to perform for extrinsic motivation rather than for your own internal motivation. You've been trained to be successful and to measure that success by outside standards, such as your income, your status in your company or work field, or your acceptance by others. All of this takes you away from being connected to yourself, to your own intrinsic movement and direction as a spiritual being. This is a form of psychic slavery, and it is extremely powerful. In psychic slavery, your masters have your mind and beliefs enslaved so that they don't even have to support you physically. They have trained you to do that yourself as well as to direct the fruits of your labors to others' designs.

This only works if your feeling nature and your heart are shut down. So you have been trained to do that, too. Now I and others—many others—are suggesting to you a whole different course. And it is founded in feeling and awakening the heart on the basis of feeling. This is the platform that will reconnect you to the entire kingdom of God. Would you like this? Do you believe it's possible?

I ask you to explore this arena and to find out for yourself. I trust this process implicitly. Your heart is of God, and it will not misguide you. You can trust it.

Much you have been taught through your institutions will fall away if you awaken your heart and begin to follow its wisdom.

Your institutions of government, religion, business, education, social control and justice, war and defense, finance, media, news and entertainment—so many of these have been corrupted and are infiltrated with beliefs and ideas that do not support you, that suppress your life and your well-being for the benefit of a few. In truth, even these few do not actually benefit because none are truly free or in joy if this occurs at the expense of others. But they do not yet know this, and so they suffer, too, as well as you. All suffer this system, this paradigm, and all are supported by any who break free of it, even though that freedom may seem threatening to those who still believe in the system and look to it for their security and safety.

I call you to be a warrior for God and for peace. And this begins within yourself, by breaking free of the shackles that have been placed on your ability to feel and connect with your heart. This is where the work is to be done. Once you connect with your heart, it becomes a journey of love that God directs. I call you to join this journey. Each one who does supports all in this path because we are all connected. All of you matter. Your choices matter. You can support the old system of control and subservience by shutting down your feeling nature and your connection to God, or you can support the path of freedom by engaging your feeling and loving connection to God through your heart. In every moment, you have a choice, and the choice happens through feeling.

I and so many others are calling to you to join us in the River of Love that flows from your heart. It is a place of great joy and love and peace. It is the place of connection with God, of growing in God, of being guided by God, of living in God, of living as God, of knowing all as God. I do not know of anything more wonderful than that. I call to you and invite you to join us in this great and wondrous process of living in and as God. I do this because I love you, because I know you as God. And I am not different from you. This is your destiny, too.

In love and service and joy,
I AM Mary Magdalene

*A*s I received this communication and listened to Mary's tone of unmistakable finality and closure, I knew I was being given her last message in this series; she sounded as if she was passing the baton to all of us, calling us to action in response to her instruction. Each time I read her words, I'm reminded of Joan of Arc, courageously leading the French soldiers into battle. But Mary's campaign is a different kind of battle: It's a battle against the forces that work to suppress our hearts. While her earlier communications address our internal structures of oppression, this one focuses on the external manifestations of oppression in our world.

Mary begins by summarizing the essence of the path of the heart: "Open your heart, feel from your heart, live from your heart. Let your mind be in service to your heart." Yet, in order to do this, we must regain our capacity for feeling, which is why she addresses the forces in the world that make this so difficult. These are our external challenges—what we must overcome and ultimately change in order to live from our hearts.

Most of us learned to suppress our feelings as children, first from our parents and later from the education system. We were told that our feelings were wrong, shamed for expressing them, distracted from them, and trained to develop our mental faculties at the expense of feeling. But we were never educated in the emotional dimension. We were taught to devalue feeling as a part of a deliberate system of control that prepares us for a life of servitude; then we learned to obey authorities rather than follow our own hearts and desires.

Mary asks us to remember a time when we were still connected to our dreams and our passions, when we believed in ourselves and our ability to manifest our desires. For me, this conjures up childhood memories of endless hours spent acting out different archetypes—mother, teacher, explorer, actress, pirate, nurse, shopkeeper, and on and on—imagining what I would be when I grew up. On washdays, when the sheets were stripped from my bed, I felt particularly inspired to animate my two favorite roles: queen and prima ballerina. Those sheets would magically transform into mythical clothing and drapery as I became the majestic characters of my dreams. This kind of play isn't just the passing whimsy of a child. Rather, when we use our imagination, we connect to an essential part of us, the part rooted in feeling and the natural drive to create and manifest, which has its source in our feeling.

Sadly, we've largely lost our ability to embrace and believe in that part of ourselves. Instead, we've been programmed since childhood to do what we were told was right and conditioned through all sorts of rewards and punishments, including praise and reprimands; grades and report cards, stars, treats, and privileges; physical punishments or social exclusion; and the use of embarrassment, guilt, shame, and threats—all to control and shape us to the will of others. Through these behavioral controls, we learned to override and abandon our own internal motivation.

Later, as adults, this conditioning continued through a system of reward and punishment—the carrots of salaries, bonuses, job security, approval, and social status, and the sticks of fines and prison—with the validity of this system constantly reinforced through mass-media messages. The result is what Mary calls psychic slavery.

In this form of slavery, people don't need to be physically coerced because they've already been indoctrinated to obey and perform. To be effective, the initial indoctrination requires extensive programming from an early age, but ultimately psychic slavery is cheaper and more convenient than physical slavery.

Perhaps at this point you're thinking, *This is too extreme. Rules and consequences are necessary for a society to function. And people need motivation in order to cooperate.* I would answer that agreements are necessary, but they don't have to come at the expense of people's internal connection to their feelings, dreams, and directions. People need motivation, but our motivation should come from within. Internal motivation is the great casualty of the system of social obedience to authority under which most of us operate. Our internal motivation gets quashed, and it's a huge loss. We lose our connection to ourselves and our aliveness, and ultimately to God. Mary wants to help us heal this loss by guiding us back to life through resurrecting our capacity for feeling.

We can remain connected to ourselves and our internal motivation and still cooperate with others. But because we have such limited experience of doing this, it's a challenge for most of us to even imagine this possibility. What if we weren't conditioned to behave in certain ways? What if, instead, we were supported in identifying and manifesting our inner divine qualities? Would this result in social chaos and destruction?

I don't believe it would. Human beings are innately caring; our inner divine qualities include caring for others and their inner divine qualities. Most people who hurt others do so because they were taught that their own inner divine qualities didn't matter and because they didn't experience others caring for their well-being and the well-being of others. Such individuals get hurt and eventually hurt others. This is what happens when people are trained to act based on rules, rewards, and punishments instead of being responded to with feeling from the heart. By contrast, people who experience care for their well-being don't need an elaborate system of reward and punishment manipulating them to behave—they're naturally moved to care for the well-being of others.

Mary urges us to reverse our life-estranging programming in order to return to our natural state of living, which is based on feeling and responding from our hearts. She says that the heart is of God, and it will not mislead us. Our hearts may, however, inspire us to radically change the structure of our world; this could mean challenging bastions of authority and control, such as religion, finance and business, political governance, judicial systems, military and defense, education, and mass media. These institutions are the outer reflections of our inner imprisonment. As we become free of our limiting beliefs about *the way things have to be*, I believe we'll see new life-serving forms and structures emerge to handle our social needs—for spiritual community and support, exchange of goods and resources, cooperation, safety, learning, communication, entertainment, and many others—in heart-based, inclusive, and co-creative ways.

Mary implores us, as warriors for God and peace, to break free of the shackles on our hearts. She beckons to us to begin the journey of love through our feeling hearts and into the kingdom of God. And she declares that she trusts this process implicitly. When we make this journey for ourselves, we make it for everyone. Because we're all interconnected, everyone is affected by our choices. Each time we choose to open to our feelings, we support everyone in their path of opening to God. Mary gives a beautiful picture of a River of Love that flows from our hearts. Whenever we open our hearts, we join the river. And each time we do this, the river grows, for ourselves and for all.

Mary ends her communication with a moving account of this River of Love. I celebrate her description and can think of no better way to close than to savor her words again:

> I and so many others are calling to you to join us in the River of Love that flows from your heart. It is a place of great joy and love and peace. It is the place of connection with God, of growing in God, of being guided by God, of living in God, of living as God, of knowing all as God. I do not know of anything more wonderful than that. I call to you and invite you to join us in this great and wondrous process of living in and as God. I do this because I love you, because I know you as God. And I am not different from you. This is your destiny, too.

Thank you, Mary, for your love and guidance. Thank you for your vision and clarity. Thank you for your trust in this process and in us. Thank you for your compassion and caring. Thank you for sharing yourself with us so fully and openly. Thank you for your joy and ecstasy in God. It has made a difference for us all.

About the Author

MERCEDES KIRKEL is a spiritual teacher who brings forth messages from Mary Magdalene and other beings of light. Mercedes is frequently published in the *Sedona Journal of Emergence!* and the *Light Circle Ezine*. She also regularly shares the messages she receives in her online newsletter, entitled *Into the Heart*. All messages and practices are universal and unaffiliated with any particular religion.

Mercedes lives in Santa Fe, New Mexico, where she offers workshops and private sessions. She also works long distance by phone and Skype, and travels to other locations upon request.

To learn more about the author, her current programs, and her upcoming books—including e-books and audiobooks—or to receive the *Into the Heart* newsletter, please visit:

www.marymagdalenebeckons.com

To purchase additional copies of *Mary Magdalene Beckons*,
in book, e-book, or audiobook format, please visit:

INTO THE HEART
Creations

www.marymagdalenebeckons.com

Made in the USA
San Bernardino, CA
21 December 2013